of Blood

PETER ACKROYD

LONDON, NEW YORK, MUNICH,
MELBOURNE and DELHI

Managing editor Andrew Macintyre
Managing art editor Jane Thomas
Senior editor Fran Jones
Senior art editor Stefan Podhorodecki
Art editors Jo Connor, Leah Germann,
Jo Little, Floyd Sayers
Publishing manager Caroline Buckingham
Publishing director Jonathan Metcalf
Production controller Rochelle Talary
Picture researchers Sean Hunter
DTP designer Siu Yin Ho
Jacket designer Neal Cobourne

Consultants
David Murdoch
Mark Jamieson

First American Edition, 2004

Published in the United States by
DK Publishing, Inc.
375 Hudson Street
New York, NY 10014

A Cataloging-in-Publication record for this book is
available from the Library of Congress.

ISBN 0-7566-1367-1

Reproduced in the UK by
Media, Development and Printing, Ltd.
Printed and bound in China by L. Rex Printing Company

Discover more at
www.dk.com

Contents

This is an account of the peoples and cultures of what we call the "new world."

But this area of the world is not new at all. It is very old. Over a period of 3,000 years or more, civilizations rose and fell in the middle and south of the Americas, unknown to the rest of the world. This is their story. It is a story of patterns that seem to be repeated throughout human history. Wandering people, hunters or gatherers, gradually become settled in one place, where they sow crops or rear animals. Small villages become larger settlements. These settlements become small towns that, in turn, grow into cities. Out of these cities there emerges one larger city that becomes a city-state with power over all the areas around it.

In the villages, there is generally a space laid aside for religious ritual and sacrifice. Then a small dwelling made of thatch and mud is built upon that sacred space. That is followed by a temple of stone, which is joined by other, possibly more elaborate, temples. There develops a powerful religious community that becomes the very center of the city. It is the heart of the city and its people. With cities, too, there emerges a division between the rich and the poor, the strong and the weak, the powerful and the less powerful. By the time these great societies have arisen, they are controlled by powerful kings with complete control over their people.

There arose many great cultures during this time—the Olmec, the Zapotec, the Toltec, the Maya, the Aztec, and the Inca. Some never had any contact with the outside world, living and dying unknown. Some still remain mysterious, the ruins of their cities hidden by vast jungles. But we know more about them now. They were based upon power and authority. They wanted to grow ever larger and, to this end, they were engaged in perpetual warfare. City fought against city, civilization fought against civilization. Warfare became an end in itself. The great cultures of the Aztecs and the Inca, for example, seemed obsessed with death. The people who lived in these societies were highly organized and tightly controlled. They believed in building stone monuments as a symbol of their power. Their religions, which dominated life and death, were fierce and warlike.

These various empires rose and fell like waves of the sea. Sometimes one emerged as another came to an end. But the empires did all come to an end. Some died in mysterious episodes of violence and destruction. Some were abandoned by their peoples, who moved on. Some were defeated by Spanish invaders. But some of the cultures survived. The Zapotecs still live where their ancestors lived almost 3,000 years ago. The Maya, whose cities were destroyed 1,000 years ago, still eat the same food and worship many of the same gods as their long-dead ancestors. So this is a story of life as well as death, of survival as well as ruin.

CHAPTER ONE

The first
sacred sites

For hundreds of years, powerful rulers and sophisticated civilizations rose and fell across Central America. Some rulers were murdered, and many cities were destroyed. The Olmecs, with their sacred sites and colossal statues, were the first of these civilizations.

THERE WAS ONCE AN AREA of the world that was the home of many kingdoms. There were many rulers and many great civilizations here, but they all shared certain beliefs and practices. They practiced human sacrifice as a means of pleasing their gods. They cut themselves so that blood flowed as an act of religious devotion. They consumed the flesh of other men and women, and also bred a type of small dog for food. They played a violent and sacred ball game. They built massive pyramids with temples on top. They designed great cities, and constructed an elaborate double calendar. How did such extraordinary cultures come to exist? These are the people of that area of the world that is now known as Mesoamerica or Central America.

◀ Temple of the Magician, Uxmal, Mexico

AREA OF MESOAMERICA
The land of the people known as Mesoamericans lies across five modern-day countries. They built their cities inland as well as along the coasts.

As its name suggests, this region is situated midway between North America and South America, and includes modern-day Mexico and Guatemala together with parts of Belize, El Salvador, and Honduras. It is a large area of great contrasts, made up of highlands and lowlands, valleys and plains, lakes and mountains, volcanoes and forests. The temperatures here vary from extreme cold to tropical heat. It is the home of the jaguar and the howler monkey, the deer and the tapir, the parrot and the hummingbird.

Some experts think that the first inhabitants migrated from Asia into North America across a bridge of land that has since been covered by a strip of sea known as the Bering Strait. Other experts think that these early people may have arrived in primitive boats. These first cultures were much like those in other parts of the world—tribes of hunter-gatherers who, as their name suggests, survived by hunting the animals around them and by eating the fruit and plants growing naturally in the areas through which they wandered. Among other creatures, they hunted the horse and the mammoth, both of which eventually became extinct in the region.

This nomadic way of life gradually gave way to more permanent settlement when the earliest Mesoamericans began to settle in areas of land that they cultivated. They were the first farmers of the region, and their crops included corn, beans, and squash. Villages emerged, at first based upon family groups who began

BIG HUNTERS
The first people in this area of the world survived by hunting wild animals, such as the mammoth. They ate the flesh and wore the animal skins to keep out the cold.

to domesticate plants and grow crops. We know these villages existed from the evidence of simple pottery, of stones for grinding corn, of woven mats and baskets.

This simple farming life remained the basis for all the great and extraordinary civilizations that were to flourish in this region. It is the central way of life for Mesoamerica and continues to this day. Other evidence of a more unusual nature has also been found. At one site, the remains of two children were discovered in an unusual position that suggests human sacrifice. In another site, known as Gheo-Shih, there are signs of an open area used for dancing or perhaps for ball games. This evidence shows that key features of a culture can be found in the very early stages of its development.

After a while, certain villages or settlements began to cluster together—for the sake of defense or for the sharing of skills. These larger villages grew naturally into small towns. One settlement might dominate a region of smaller settlements, and as this grew into a larger community, it needed to be better organized. Roles and duties were divided between different people—the skills of the stronger and the smarter were recognized. Certain forms of magical religion were also established, conducted by a spiritual leader, called a shaman, who had special powers. Archaeologists have found evidence, in these larger settlements, of public spaces and of communal buildings. There are the remnants of luxury goods, such as mirrors and objects made of jade.

One such large settlement is Tlatilco, where an extensive burial ground has revealed the remains of decorated and sculpted

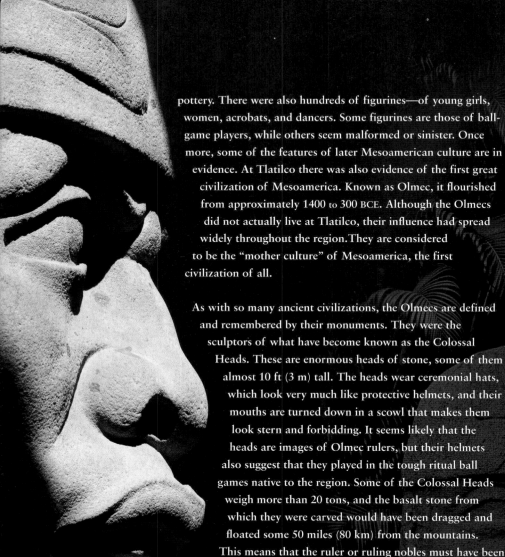

pottery. There were also hundreds of figurines—of young girls, women, acrobats, and dancers. Some figurines are those of ball-game players, while others seem malformed or sinister. Once more, some of the features of later Mesoamerican culture are in evidence. At Tlatilco there was also evidence of the first great civilization of Mesoamerica. Known as Olmec, it flourished from approximately 1400 to 300 BCE. Although the Olmecs did not actually live at Tlatilco, their influence had spread widely throughout the region. They are considered to be the "mother culture" of Mesoamerica, the first civilization of all.

As with so many ancient civilizations, the Olmecs are defined and remembered by their monuments. They were the sculptors of what have become known as the Colossal Heads. These are enormous heads of stone, some of them almost 10 ft (3 m) tall. The heads wear ceremonial hats, which look very much like protective helmets, and their mouths are turned down in a scowl that makes them look stern and forbidding. It seems likely that the heads are images of Olmec rulers, but their helmets also suggest that they played in the tough ritual ball games native to the region. Some of the Colossal Heads weigh more than 20 tons, and the basalt stone from which they were carved would have been dragged and floated some 50 miles (80 km) from the mountains. This means that the ruler or ruling nobles must have been able to muster a large work-force for collective activities, a further indication of a powerful civilization.

COLOSSAL HEADS
This is one of 17 heads discovered in Mexico. Historians think that the Olmecs carved them 3,000 years ago. A flat nose, almond-shaped eyes, and full lips feature on all the heads.

Another famous Olmec image is that of a child and jaguar mixed together as if it were part-human and part-animal. These images generally take the form of an infant that has the snarl and facial features of a jaguar. They are known as were-jaguars, just as other hybrid creatures are known as werewolves. The significance of these images is not entirely clear, although the Olmec creation myth suggests that human life sprang out of these strange creatures.

The Olmecs had three main regional centers. One site, known as San Lorenzo, is a human-made mound more than half a mile (1 km) long and over 150 ft (45 m) tall. It would have required enormous labor and energy, as well as planning, to build such a monument. It is designed symmetrically—with one half a mirror image of the other—and is believed to represent a gigantic bird. Seventy monumental sculptures were found on the mound—among them ten Colossal Heads, as well as great stone altars, probably used as thrones for the Olmec rulers. A pyramid structure was found on this plateau as well as a long, rectangular court. This was a center of religious ritual and ceremony. Religion is often the principal form of power in ancient societies where there is no strong military base. San Lorenzo and the other main Olmec religious center, La Venta, seem to have exerted control over a significantly large territory.

San Lorenzo was a place to live as well as a place to worship. Palatial dwellings were found near its summit, and poorer dwellings at a lower level for the working population. The workshops of the stonemasons, who labored over the hard basalt stone, have also been found here. Perhaps more surprising, however, was the

JADE JEWELRY
This necklace with a human head at its center would have been worn by a member of the elite, such as a ruler or a priest. Green stones were valued more than any other material in Mesoamerica.

WERE-JAGUARS
The combination of a child's face with a jaguar's had great meaning for the Olmecs. The jaguar was a common creature in Central America and represented strength and association with the gods.

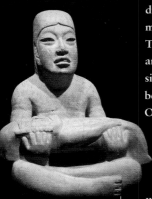

discovery of a system of waterways—a line of stone blocks that may have acted as an aqueduct, channeling water to the sacred sites. The basalt used in the creation of Olmec monuments came from another regional center known as Laguna de los Cerros. This was situated near the Tuxtla Mountains, where the basalt was quarried before being floated down a network of waterways to the other Olmec settlements. Historians think that the basalt may have been carved at Laguna de los Cerros and the completed sculptures transported around the region.

Evidence of an Olmec community was also found at La Venta, which was built on an island in the midst of the coastal swamps, and after its demise remained hidden for centuries among the tropical vegetation like some lost world. Here were large courts or plazas, encircled by platform mounds, and a pyramid mound rising more

SACRED BABIES
This is a typical Olmec statue with the priest showing the same facial features as the Colossal Heads. The act of carrying a baby was sacred to the Olmecs, and is depicted in many of their sculptures.

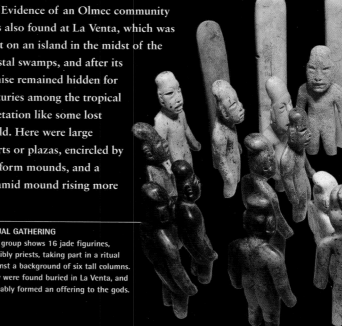

RITUAL GATHERING
This group shows 16 jade figurines, possibly priests, taking part in a ritual against a background of six tall columns. They were found buried in La Venta, and probably formed an offering to the gods.

than 100 ft (30 m). Within this pyramid several royal burials were found, together with scowling masks, jewelry, and figurines of polished jade. These figurines were executed with great artistry, but in certain respects they remain quite mysterious. Some of them show human figures in contorted shapes. There are also examples of shape-shifting, with the human figure turning into a jaguar. Part of the head is turned into that of a big cat. These further examples of the were-jaguar have suggested to historians that they represent aspects of the shaman's religious rites. He may have ritually "turned" into an animal god, or been invested with the divine essence of a god.

There are signs of the Olmec faith everywhere. Some evidence suggests that human sacrifice was an aspect of their religion. The discovery of a number of heads buried separately from their bodies implies, at the very least, less than natural deaths. The spine of a stingray was unearthed; this sharp instrument was generally used for the ritual piercing of the tongue or more private parts to produce blood. There are many human bones that have been burned and scraped, suggesting that the Olmecs could be cannibals on occasions. This act of eating flesh is an enduring aspect of Mesoamerican ritual

ANIMAL GODS
Many animals were used to represent Olmec gods, including jaguars, eagles, and monkeys. The open, snarling mouth of this figure is typical of the spirit of the jaguar. The cleft head is another way to show an Olmec god.

THE WRESTLER
El Luchador, or The Wrestler, is an unusual Olmec statue because it shows a man in action, instead of a static pose. His facial hair of mustache and beard is unusual and may have been added to symbolize someone of noble birth.

And at La Venta, once more, there are tokens of the ritual ball games practiced throughout the region. Seven rubber balls have been found, ranging in size from a modern tennis ball to a basketball. As we will see later, these were sacred and sometimes murderous games. But the violence was not confined to the ball court. From pictorial evidence, it seems likely that the Olmecs fought against neighboring tribes, wielding clubs equipped with blades of flint or obsidian (glassy volcanic rock). They also used a kind of sharp instrument attached to the knuckles of the hand.

It is significant that the Olmecs invented a form of writing. It could, in fact, be said that they introduced writing to this part of the world. Their script is a form of picture writing, like the hieroglyphs of the ancient Egyptians. They also created a calendar, based on a mixture of mathematics and of astronomy. For the first time in the history of the Americas, a system of counting was developed by means of bars and dots. In this system, a dot represents one, and a bar represents five.

DEADLY WEAPONS
A range of deadly weapons, such as clubs and knives, were made from obsidian and used in ritual killing as well as war. Obsidian was glasslike rock that could be fashioned into a blade.

So it is possible to begin to recognize all the elements of a civilization growing out of what were once small farming settlements. A religion emerged, a system where people were ranked according to status emerged, a form of early writing also emerged. There were wars and games, trade and sacrifice. The precise sequence of events, over a period of thousands of years, cannot now be recovered. But it is clear enough that the binding force, which drew in other settlements and villages, was the power of sacred beliefs. From the heat of the tropical forests, forms of violent ritual arose, calling up the spirits of the serpent and of the jaguar. There was a corn god, too, and supernatural dwarves who lived in waterfalls. There were shamans who were possessed by the gods, and who spoke of divine things. Human victims were killed and eaten.

Like most other Mesoamerican cultures, the Olmec civilization died in some violent cataclysm. The altars were damaged. The statues of the rulers were defaced. The ritual centers were deserted. There have been many explanations for this sudden demise, ranging from the weakening effects of some epidemic disease to an invasion by alien tribes. It also seems possible that the Olmec people destroyed their own culture, perhaps even aided by their priests and rulers, in a kind of ritual destruction, the purposes of which are unclear. The rest is silence.

POWER OF A SHAMAN
A shaman was a spiritual leader in Olmec society. Here, he is shown sitting on the stomach of a great snake. In his hand, he carries a small bag that may contain the special herbs he would use to banish bad spirits from a person or place.

CHAPTER TWO

Cities
of stone

From the landscapes of Central America there arose
great cities of stone whose presence announced the
emergence of a new order. This was most evident from
the imposing pyramids, the rise of the warrior class,
and the cult of the legendary god Quetzalcoatl.

I T IS A STRIKING FEATURE OF the ancient Mesoamerican world that great cultures flourished even as others died or were brought back to life. While the Olmec center at La Venta continued to thrive, another great city culture emerged much farther south in the valley of the Oaxaca. This was the region of the people who became known as the Zapotecs because they lived in an area where many zapote trees grew. The great city of the Zapotec is known as Monte Alban. It was built on an easy-to-defend hilltop that towered high above the valley floor and enjoyed panoramic views of the surrounding countryside. Monte Alban survived for well over a thousand years, and at the height of its power was inhabited by as many as 20,000 people. It is remarkable that the descendants of those Zapotecs still live in the area.

◀ Serpent head of Quetzalcoatl at Teotihuacan

In order to build the sacred center of the city, a massive workforce flattened an entire mountaintop—a truly enormous undertaking. When completed, the city center boasted many features typical of Mesoamerican civilization. There was a ball court with slanting sides. There were temples and palaces, pyramids and public spaces for rituals. The nobles and the priests lived within the city center itself, while members of the community who were considered less important lived in homes built of mud and thatch on the terraces of the hillside. It seems that the more favored you were, the closer you lived to the center of sacred power.

One of the most fascinating structures within the city is known as the Temple of the Dancers. It was given that name because it is decorated with 300 stone images of human figures in strange positions, as if they were taking part in some hysterical dance. In fact, they are not dancers at all—they are corpses, and their postures and attitudes are now interpreted as those of the dead. Experts think that the Zapotec were portraying the images of their dead enemies who had been slain in battle or as a result of some ritual sacrifice.

AN ANGRY GOD
This sculpted clay head shows the face of Cocijo, the Zapotec rain god. "Cocijo" is Zapotec for "lightning," and the face of the god is meant to show the powerful and angry face of the sky.

This theme of war is reflected elsewhere in Monte Alban. One great structure was built in the shape of an arrowhead—a symbol of threat and aggression. In fact, records of Zapotec military victories were carved into some 50 stone slabs found within the structure. It is almost as if the Zapotecs had constructed a center with buildings that were designed to announce how powerful and strong the city and its people were. But this arrowhead structure may have had another purpose. Archaeologists have found evidence of a sight tube here, which suggests that the building may have been used as an observatory from which to view the stars. If this was the case, it would have been the first observatory ever built in Mesoamerica. It seems likely that these distant civilizations understood that their world was part of some vast universe.

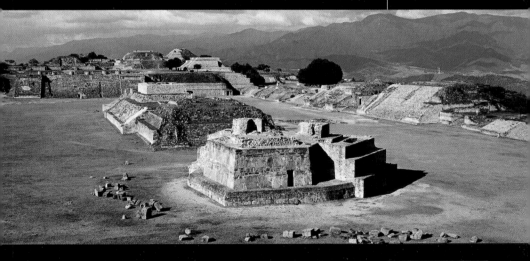

Yet the power of Monte Alban was, in the end, overtaken by the greatest of all Mesoamerican cities—a city that the Aztecs later referred to as "the city of the gods." The name of the people who built and inhabited Teotihuacan is not known. It is still a mysterious civilization that rose and fell without leaving any clue to its origin. Experts do know that, for a while at least, this was the largest city in the western hemisphere. It covered some 8 square miles (20 sq km)—larger than Rome at the height of its imperial power—and was populated

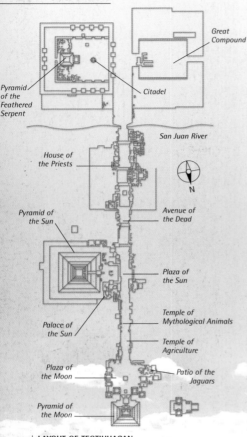

Great
Compound

Pyramid
of the
Feathered
Serpent

Citadel

San Juan River

House of
the Priests

N

Pyramid of
the Sun

Avenue of
the Dead

Plaza of
the Sun

Temple of
Mythological Animals

Palace of
the Sun

Temple of
Agriculture

Plaza of
the Moon

Patio of the
Jaguars

Pyramid of
the Moon

LAYOUT OF TEOTIHUACAN
Building Teotihuacan was a massive task. During its
construction, the San Juan River was diverted to flow
across the Avenue of the Dead and divide the city in four.
This map shows the Avenue running north to south.

by some 200,000 people at its peak in 500 CE.
It was given the name Teotihuacan, and it lasted
for approximately 800 years, until its temples
were defaced and destroyed in an unexplained
act of violence or vengeance.

The people of Teotihuacan worshiped the Rain
God and the Feathered Serpent and a strange
divinity known as Our Lord the Flayed One.
These are the gods that would come to dominate
all the great city-states of the region. Yet the
ruling god of Teotihuacan itself was none of
these. She was a fearsome being known as the
Spider Woman, who was portrayed with the
fangs of a spider. The city was built as a center
for the worship of these gods and was divided
into four great quadrants. The main dividing line
was a wide thoroughfare, known as the Avenue
of the Dead, which stretched for some 2 miles
(3 km) through the middle of the city. The avenue
formed a wide processional way lined with altars
and temples, platforms and dwelling places.

GRISLY REMAINS
Rows of skeletons were found in Teotihuacan grave sites. These are probably the remains of victims sacrificed at the dedication ceremony of the Pyramid of the Feathered Serpent.

Walking north you would pass the Pyramid of the Feathered Serpent, and then, farther north, the Pyramid of the Sun, before you reached a great plaza laid out before the Pyramid of the Moon. This would have been one of the main places in the city for performing sacred rituals.

The city seems to have been created as a piece of living geography, with pyramids built to mirror the mountains in the distance. If you stood at a certain point on the Avenue of the Dead, the tip of the Pyramid of the Moon lined up exactly with the top of the Cerro Gordo mountain, which dominated the surrounding landscape. The entire city was an astonishing construction that rivaled anything in ancient Greece or Rome. The Pyramid of the Sun was the third-largest pyramid ever built, and can be compared with the great pyramids of the Egyptian pharaohs. Its great size was an indication of the power of the rulers of Teotihuacan, who could marshal the labor of thousands of individuals to help them build their vision out of stones. Excavations by archaeologists have revealed much about how these pyramids were constructed. It seems that workers

AVENUE OF THE DEAD
This view of the Avenue of the Dead, with the Pyramid of the Sun (left), is shown from the steps of the Pyramid of the Moon. In the foreground is the great Plaza of the Moon. All the buildings in the city were painted, many with scenes from mythology.

built up many small rooms or cells out of pieces of rock, then filled the space inside the cells with more rocks and mud. Eventually all the cells would have been connected, then another layer built on top, and so on until the pyramid reached its full height. The whole structure would then have been faced with stone slabs. It is estimated that 1,300,000 cubic yards (1,000,000 cubic meters) of rocks and mud were used to build the Pyramid of the Sun.

Deep within the Pyramid of the Sun lies a shrine. This was a natural cave and, before the pyramid was ever built, would probably have been a place of worship. Throughout Mesoamerica, people believed that caves were gateways for the gods, as well as a point of entry to the underworld where demons and other powerful beings reigned supreme. This particular cave could have been significant because it had four chambers, which reflected the idea that the universe was divided into four quadrants. The people of Teotihuacan probably believed that the gods once emerged from this cave, so they erected a pyramid on the site. And then, at a later date, another pyramid was built to cover the original. The Pyramid of the Moon, close by, contains the forms of six

BEHIND THE MASK
Teotihuacanos covered the faces of their dead with burial masks. This mask has a mosaic pattern of turquoise and coral around the nose. The pupils are fashioned from obsidian.

other pyramids built on the same spot at earlier dates. It appears that the original buildings were in a literal sense buried, almost as if they were human.

The third pyramid at Teotihuacan, the Pyramid of the Feathered Serpent, is not as large as its two companions, but it does possess one remarkable feature. The ritual human sacrifice of hundreds of people accompanied its erection. The body of one victim was placed at each corner of the pyramid, and a large number were found lodged at its center. Drawings made by archaeologists show these victims with their knees drawn up and their arms outstretched. This makes them look like dancing skeletons—very much like the stone images of the "dancers" found at Monte Alban.

There were palaces in the city for the nobler and the richer inhabitants, and these were decorated with finely crafted murals of human figures and animals. But, perhaps more interestingly, there were also complexes of "apartments" in walled compounds. These apartments were made up of many separate rooms grouped around a central courtyard, complete with small temples for worship. It has been estimated that between 50 and 100 people lived in each apartment complex. They may have been grouped by trade or by family ties, but whatever their precise organization, these arrangements suggest that many of the people had become true city-dwellers, far removed from their farming roots.

PYRAMID OF THE SUN
The skyline of the city was dominated by the largest pyramid in Mesoamerica—the Pyramid of the Sun. It stood 207 ft (63 m) tall with each of the four square sides measuring 722 ft (220 m). A tunnel under the pyramid leads to caves that were once used for religious ceremonies.

The principal trade of the city workers was probably the manufacture of small statues and pottery as well as the preparation and export of obsidian, which was widely used to make weapons. In return, the city imported cotton and rubber as well as luxury products such as feathers, shells, and precious stones from the surrounding countryside. A giant market, situated off the Avenue of the Dead, would have been the bustling hub of everyday life in the city. Here, everything from painted pots and live parrots to fresh fish and feathered ornaments would have been traded. The demand for corn, squash, and cacao beans and all the other staples of life must have placed an enormous burden on the resources of the region under the supervision of Teotihuacan.

The existence of a calendar and a system for writing would have greatly supported the development of trade—writing, to help with record-keeping, and a calendar so that accurate dates and times could be calculated. A calendar had been developed, as well as a form of writing by means of glyphs. These glyphs are essentially marks or symbols cut into stone. If Mesoamerican cities were centers of religious ritual, they were also great powerhouses of human energy, which imposed order upon their surroundings.

Despite all this, the city was deliberately destroyed during the 8th century CE, its main temples burned and its palaces vandalized. Its people may have risen up in revolt against their priests and rulers. The city may have fallen to invaders, or it may have perished because of food shortages. No one can be sure. The demise of Teotihuacan was part of a general pattern of instability in Mesoamerica. Other great cities, such as Monte Alban, also fell in the general decline. Yet other city states rose to take their place. It has been suggested that much of the instability

PARROTS FOR SALE
The brightly colored feathers of parrots, macaws, and quetzal birds were considered luxuries. The wealthy bought these feathers to decorate mural paintings and ornaments.

TYPICAL FOOD
Staple foods such as corn, squash, and cacao beans were all sold in the market of Teotihuacan. In Aztec times, cacao beans were used as a form of money.

at the time sprang from the migration of tribes who had to fight their way through different territories as they moved south. The invasion of these tribes may have led religious societies to be replaced by more militaristic societies. The warrior class became more important than the priestly castes, and the cities became more heavily fortified and defended. There is no better example of this military culture than the rise of a people known as the Toltecs. In legendary accounts, they were taken southward by a leader called Mixcoatl, or Cloud Serpent. Mixcoatl became a god after his death but not before he had given birth to a son, who took the name Quetzalcoatl, or Feathered Serpent. Quetzalcoatl was said to have founded the city of Tula, which would become the home of the Toltecs.

The city of Tula was first inhabited by the Toltecs in the 10th century CE. It covered almost 6 square miles (15 sq km) and

PYRAMID OF QUETZALCOATL
Images of the Feathered Serpent are commonplace in Mesoamerica. This serpent head is from the Pyramid of Quetzalcoatl in Teotihuacan.

The legend of Quetzalcoatl

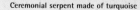
Ceremonial serpent made of turquoise

Quetzalcoatl, also known as the Feathered Serpent, was a Toltec god who founded the city of Tula. He encouraged peace but was challenged by a magician called Tezcatlipoca, or Smoking Mirror, who preferred sacrifice and war. Using sorcery, the magician expelled him from the city, and Quetzalcoatl wandered to the Gulf of Mexico. He set fire to himself and rose into the heavens as the morning star. In another account, he set sail, promising to come back one day. In 1519, when the Aztecs saw the billowing sails of the Spanish ships, they thought it was Quetzalcoatl returning.

ON PAIN OF DEATH
A chacmool is a reclining figure used throughout Mesoamerica. Its deadly task was to hold a container for the hearts and blood of people sacrificed to the gods. At one time, they would have been brightly colored.

was designed like the immense city of Teotihuacan, with a grid of streets boasting palaces and temples and altars as well as dwelling-places for some 40,000 people. These dwellings were generally made up of five linked houses, with a courtyard and an altar. There were ball courts, and a large plaza containing a pyramid devoted to Quetzalcoatl. On the pyramid was a temple to the Feathered Serpent with great statues of the god by its entrance. Paintings of a serpent devouring a human body decorated the sides of the pyramid. These Toltec gods were obviously aggressive deities, just as the Toltecs seem to have been an aggressive people. Inside the temple four stone figures represented Toltec warriors. The images of warriors were carved everywhere in Tula. The widespread presence of these images suggests a predominantly militaristic society. Tula might even be described as the first military culture in Mesoamerica.

Stone figures known as chacmools were found at Tula, too. Chacmools were sculptures of death—reclining human figures with basins in their middle. The hearts torn out of the chests of sacrificial victims were placed in these bowls. There are altars on which the skulls of the dead were placed. From the evidence of domestic remains, people who died naturally in Tula were buried under the houses, but the victims of sacrifice were eaten, and their bones left in garbage dumps. The city of warfare was also the city of cannibalism and human sacrifice. But it was a city of empire, too. Although the extent of its influence is still unclear, Tula controlled most of what is now central Mexico, and its territories probably ranged from the Pacific Ocean to the Gulf of Mexico. Within its area of control were great centers producing objects made of obsidian and turquoise.

The influence of Toltec culture seems also to have spread very widely. It is likely that the Toltecs were some of the first Mesoamericans to work in metal, but more significantly, their images of serpents and their reclining chacmool figures can be found all over the area. There is a great city known as Chichén Itzá on the Yucatán Peninsula. Although probably Maya in origin, this city seems to have become a second Toltec home. It is almost 700 miles (1,100 km) from Tula, but it shares extraordinary resemblances with that city. There are many images of feathered serpents, otherwise unknown in the region, as well as images of jaguars and warriors. There are even Toltec chacmools, bearing their own clues about the practice of human sacrifice. The close connection between Tula and Chichén Itzá is not understood. These ancient empires kept many of their secrets.

The Toltec Empire, established upon violence, also died in violence. Tula existed for only 250 years before being suddenly destroyed. Its public buildings were burned to the ground, its temples desecrated, and its stone monuments toppled. It is not clear who was responsible for this, but it may have been the work of invading northern tribes. It has also been suggested that Tula was destroyed at the hands of the Aztecs, the great and fearsome tribe that now, for the first time, enters recorded history.

WARRIORS STAND GUARD
These giant stone warriors once helped to support the roof of a wood-and-thatch temple in the city of Tula. The butterfly shape on their breastplates was the symbol of a warrior. Each also has a feathered headdress.

CHAPTER THREE

Enter *the* Aztecs

No one is certain about the exact origins of the Aztecs. In their own creation myths, they claimed to have sprung from an island called Aztlán, or "Land of the White Herons." They believed they were summoned to a greater life.

T HE MYTHS OF THE AZTECS tell how they left their native home, led by the image of their god—Huitzilopochtli, or Hummingbird on the Left—carried on the shoulders of four priests. It became a kind of pilgrimage. On this long journey, Huitzilopochtli gave them the new name of Mexica, after which the modern country of Mexico is named. Through the visions of his priests, Huitzilopochtli revealed that the Mexica would become the lords of the universe, to whom the world would pay tribute in gold and precious jewels. The myths also tell that in the course of their sacred journey, the Mexica encountered the Curved Mountain known as Culhuacan and the Seven Caves of Chicomoztoc. From out of these caves came the seven tribes of the earth. In Aztec mythology, it became a place of regeneration and new life.

◀ Aztec myths refer to the "Land of the White Herons"

The most likely real origin of the Aztecs is perhaps less imaginative, but it is certainly interesting. They seem to have been among the invading tribes that traveled southward into the fertile Valley of Mexico in the 13th century. They were mostly hunters who, whenever they settled in one place for a time, took up simple forms of agriculture. They were organized in quite sophisticated tribal groupings, each with their own gods and their own rituals. However, the Aztecs were known as "the people whose face nobody knows," and it seems that they were not welcomed by the inhabitants of the regions through which they journeyed. They may have tried to settle in hospitable areas, but were always forced to move on. Sometimes they were grudgingly accepted as cheap labor, working the fields as serfs or contracted slaves. Yet even during these hard times, it should be remembered, they still believed themselves to be a chosen race, destined to rule the world.

Eventually, they settled in a place known as Chapultepec on the shore of Lake Texcoco. While they were here, they gained a reputation for violence and bravado, but by the end of the 13th century, they had been forced to move once more, this time into the land known as Culhuacan. They were not welcomed here, either. In fact, the Aztec leader was ritually sacrificed by the leaders of the Culhua people who lived at Culhuacan. This was not a good sign, but the Culhua did allow them to stay in the region—even though it was a rocky territory inhabited only by snakes and insects. The Aztecs, however, were a bold and enterprising people. Instead of fleeing this

LAND OF SNAKES
The Aztecs were never allowed to stay anywhere for long. At one point, they arrived in Culhuacan, where the ruler gave them a desolate plot in the desert that was home to many snakes.

Pachucha
Tula
Tlatelolco
Teotihuacan
Tenochtitlán ■ ▲ Mt. Tlaloc
Lake Texcoco
Mt. ▲ ● Tlaxcala
Popocatepetl
El Tajin
Quiahuitzlan
Orizaba
Gulf of Mexico
Tres Zapotes
La Venta
San Lorenzo
Monte Alban
Tehuantepec

■ Aztec cities
● Earlier cities

wasteland of ancient lava, they
made full use of it. They hunted the
snakes that were supposed to kill them. They
boiled and ate them, surviving so well that over the next few
years they began to cultivate land and build houses out of the rocks.

**KEY SITES IN
MESOAMERICA**
This map shows the
distribution of early
cities settled by the first
civilizations in the
central area of America.
It also shows locations of
the main Aztec cities.

The Culhua soon recognized the fighting skills of the Aztecs, and
they were engaged as mercenaries (hired soldiers) to help in their
battles against neighboring tribes. The Aztecs began to trade, and
marry, with the Culhua. But then, according to legend, there was a
terrible misunderstanding. The Aztecs asked for the daughter of a
Culhuan leader to become a bride of their god. A young girl was duly
presented for the marriage service, but the Aztecs promptly
sacrificed her. Her body was flayed (skinned), and her skin
draped over the shoulders of a priest. When the Culhuan leader
arrived, expecting to see his daughter happily married, he found
her flayed skin displayed in triumph. The Aztecs believed that
they had created a goddess of war, but the Culhuan leader saw
only the mutilated body of his daughter. As a result, the Aztecs
were violently expelled from the
region, and forced to take refuge in
the uninhabited areas surrounding
Lake Texcoco. They divided into
two tribes, and for some years both
groups managed to survive among
the reeds and marshes. But then one
of the tribes had a vision.

CLOAK OF SKIN
The Aztecs practiced the flaying
of skin, which involved cutting
off the skin from a sacrificial
victim. To the Aztecs, this
represented the bursting of the
skin of corn seeds. The god Xipe
Totec, also known as Our Lord
the Flayed One, is shown here
wearing a human skin.

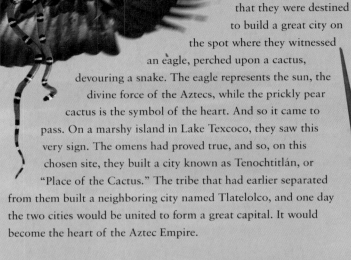

According to legend, this vision revealed that they were destined to build a great city on the spot where they witnessed an eagle, perched upon a cactus, devouring a snake. The eagle represents the sun, the divine force of the Aztecs, while the prickly pear cactus is the symbol of the heart. And so it came to pass. On a marshy island in Lake Texcoco, they saw this very sign. The omens had proved true, and so, on this chosen site, they built a city known as Tenochtitlán, or "Place of the Cactus." The tribe that had earlier separated from them built a neighboring city named Tlatelolco, and one day the two cities would be united to form a great capital. It would become the heart of the Aztec Empire.

At first, Tenochtitlán was a modest settlement for the Mexica, made up of huts built from the reeds that grew all around them. Its inhabitants scraped together a meager living. They hunted the birds and fish of the region, while the women traded in the markets along the shores of the lake. The chief of the tribe was known as Tenoch, and under his

AZTEC LEGEND
The eagle and the snake are part of Aztec legend. The city of Tenochtitlán was sited where they were seen perched on a cactus.

CITY FOUNDATIONS
This Aztec drawing shows the founding of the city of Tenochtitlán. The legend of the eagle and the cactus continues today—they are the symbols on the modern Mexican flag.

leadership, the growing town began to develop a more elaborate and more sophisticated social system. The leading families of the Mexica intermarried with the nobles of other local cities, so that family ties would replace rivalry. On the death of Tenoch, his successor was chosen because of his good relationships with other tribal leaders. His name was Acamapichtli.

Even though the Mexica were growing more powerful, they still fell under the influence of a strong local tribe, which had established the first city state and empire since the time of Teotihuacan. These were the Tepanecs—under the leadership of a great ruler known as Tezozomoc. He recognized and appreciated the qualities—ferocity and hardiness—of the Mexica in battle, and he hired them as mercenaries in his army. He also placed their city under his protection. They were, for a while, his warriors, and they learned first-hand the skills they would need to create and keep an empire.

But they were not to be kept under Tepanec control for very long. Under the leadership of one of Acamapichtli's successors, Itzcoatl, the Mexica decided to fight

WINNER TAKES ALL
The Aztecs loved gambling, and a favorite game was *patolli*. Players sat a round a cross-shaped mat and threw beans instead of dice. Slaves, jewels, and homes were all gambled on the outcome of the game.

their overlords. Many of them were afraid of the consequences, but the leaders offered them a bet. The bet ran as follows. If we are victorious, then the commoners will agree to serve and obey us. If we are unsuccessful against the Tepanec, then the commoners can take their revenge "and devour us in dirty and broken pots." Once more, we sense the literally bloodthirsty ideas of this tribe—a tribe who represented their sun god as a face with its tongue hanging out, thirsty for human blood.

LOCUST SWARMS
When huge swarms of locusts descended on the Aztec crops, there was havoc. The food supplies were wiped out almost instantly and people starved to death.

The bet was successful. The Aztecs formed a league with two other cities, defeated the Tepanec in battle, and ritually sacrificed their leader. The Aztecs would become by far the strongest of the allies who fought the Tepanec. They had shaken off their old masters, and would go on to dominate their neighbors as well as more distant territories. Itzcoatl himself was perhaps the first great leader of the Aztecs. With the help of his nephew, the high priest Tlacaelel, he forged the identity of his people. He created the Aztecs. The history of the people was set down. The principles of the religion were organized into clearly defined codes or rules. Aztec society itself was overhauled. It seems that, under the guidance of Tlacaelel, human sacrifice was granted an ever more prominent place in religious rituals.

Itzcoatl was the *tlatoani*, or great leader, of the Aztecs. *Tlatoani* means, literally, "he who speaks." Itzcoatl was succeeded in 1440 by one of his former advisers, Moctezuma, who embarked upon a program of imperial conquest. During Moctezuma's reign, the Aztec Empire began to feel its strength. In the early years, his task was to

AGRICULTURE
The Aztecs worked hard to plant and harvest corn (top two images). They used digging sticks to cultivate the land. Another crop, amaranth (bottom image), was also used because it ripened before the corn did.

strengthen Aztec power among their immediate neighbors in the Valley of Mexico. But his work of domination was complicated by a series of disasters. There were great floods and unseasonable frosts as well as terrible famines caused by hordes of locusts that devoured all the crops. The vultures hovered in the valley above the starving Aztecs. Yet they survived to witness more successful harvests.

Feeling ever stronger, Moctezuma's armies marched into the rich and tropical regions along the Gulf of Mexico. They reached the eastern coast, and they also conquered important trading centers in the interior. They overpowered peoples scattered through the valleys, such as the Mixtecs, and brought back tribute from scores of different cities. So great was Moctezuma's success, in fact, that he proclaimed that his birth had been miraculous and that he was himself half god, half man. His image was carved in stone, like those of the Egyptian pharaohs. In the same way as the pharaohs, he set up a family dynasty of rulers. Three of his grandsons became in turn the *tlatoani* of the Aztecs. This was the beginning of a highly organized empire, arranged in strict layers, with the king at the top of an elaborate hierarchy of warriors and priests and nobles.

FACE OF A GOD
The Mixtecs were master jewelers, making ornaments from gold, silver, and copper. This gold face, which hung on a necklace, shows Xipe Totec, patron god of all the goldsmiths.

THE KING IN HIS PALACE
This version of a scene from the *Florentine Codex* shows the king, or *tlatoani*, seated in his palace. The red scrolls coming from his mouth indicate that he is speaking. The king wears a decorated cloak and a headband as a sign of royalty.

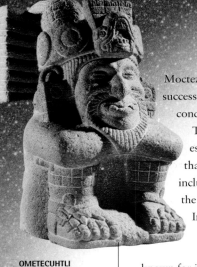

Moctezuma reigned for almost 30 years, and his immediate successor, Axayacatl, continued his tradition of blood and conquest. In particular, he brought under his power Tenochtitlán's sister city of Tlatelolco, the city that had been established by a branch of the same tribe. Despite the fact that the inhabitants of the two cities had much in common, including a shared ancestry, the leaders of Tlatelolco resented the authority of Tenochtitlán, and rose up in revolt against it. In retaliation, Axayacatl launched an expedition against them, conquered them, and plundered their city. Although Tlatelolco continued as a prosperous and thriving city, known for its riches and for its markets, it would remain under the influence of its more powerful neighbor.

Axayacatl also marched north and northwest, subjugating some 37 towns or cities in the course of his 12-year reign. But his achievements were not matched by his successor, Tizoc, who preferred monument-building to warfare. It seems that Tizoc's military efforts were devoted to suppressing rebellion in the conquered territories rather than further imperial expansion. He is reported to have captured only 14 towns, which, by Aztec standards, was a half-hearted performance. He died after a suspiciously short reign of five years, probably poisoned by his brother, the more aggressive Ahuizotl, who promptly took command.

Ahuizotl was perhaps the most successful and enterprising of all the Aztec *tlatoani*. He extended the boundaries of the

Aztec Empire throughout Mesoamerica, until it had become the largest empire in the region since the days of the Toltecs. He pushed southward until the Aztecs controlled the Pacific shores. He conquered the cities of the Zapotecs and the Mixtecs. He took control of 45 towns. He reached the borders of what is today Guatemala. He established colonies and built fortifications along the frontiers of the empire. He set up temples in other conquered regions, linking them with the religious rituals of the capital.

He also engaged in building works at home. He renovated the capital, Tenochtitlán, and rebuilt the Great Temple at the heart of the city. It is reported that during the ceremonies that marked the opening of the new temple, more than 80,000 human beings were sacrificed in just four days. Ahuizotl was the king of death as well as of war. He ripped open the victims' chests and tore out their still-beating hearts until he was exhausted. Then a priest took over his duties. The blood was like a river, streaming down the steps of the pyramid on which the temple was built. The smell of death was intense. Ambassadors from other cities were apparently appalled by such carnage, while the population could

LORD OF THE UNDERWORLD
Mictlantecuhtli, the Aztec god of death, is most often shown as a white skeleton, sometimes with bloodstains. This pottery figure shows Mictlantecuhtli grinning as he welcomes the dead to his underworld, known as Mictlan.

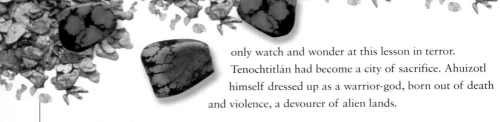

only watch and wonder at this lesson in terror. Tenochtitlán had become a city of sacrifice. Ahuizotl himself dressed up as a warrior-god, born out of death and violence, a devourer of alien lands.

TURQUOISE AND GOLD
The Aztecs greatly valued precious stones, especially turquoise. However, the ultimate symbol of wealth and power was gold. This is why Moctezuma's crown was made from a combination of turquoise and gold.

Ahuizotl ruled for 16 years, and was succeeded by the last Aztec emperor. The story of Moctezuma II's tragic confrontation with the Spaniards, and their destruction of the Aztec Empire, will be told in its proper place. Yet during the course of Moctezuma II's reign, the glory and power of the ruler reached new heights. He was called "the mother and father of the city." No one was allowed to look upon his face—if they did, they would be killed. He was carried on a litter (a couch with carrying handles) by noblemen, with a screen raised between him and the people. His feet were not permitted to touch the ground, so cloths were laid in front of him wherever he walked. He was attended by 3,000 servants. At each meal, which he ate sitting alone, a huge range of different dishes was offered to him. He wore a magnificent crown of gold decorated with turquoise stones, as well as a huge emerald in the cartilage between his two nostrils. He wore great emerald earrings, and on his arms there were bracelets and golden bells. He wore shining blue-green cloths decorated with jewels and painted with emblems, and his feet were protected by sandals made from the skins of jaguars. In his hand, he carried a scepter in the shape of a serpent. Moctezuma set up a system of ruling that relied entirely on hierarchy and order. He wished for absolute power.

FEATHERED FANS
The feathers of brightly colored birds were used in the making of elaborate fans. With a bamboo handle and a butterfly design, fans like these were only intended for leaders and emperors.

But Moctezuma had duties as well as powers. He had to pay for the continual Aztec wars. In one month of every year, he distributed food and drink to all citizens. He oversaw the great religious festivals of the kingdom, and was seen as the defender of the land. He was thought to maintain the harmony of the universe. On ritual occasions he danced before the people as a symbol of that harmony. He also had to maintain the expansion of the empire, since that was the destiny of his people. If they did not continue to conquer, the Aztec Empire would collapse. (And this is precisely what did happen at the end of his reign.) So he took over territories that had eluded his predecessor. He conquered whole tribes and captured cities, until his subjects could be counted in millions.

Of course, he relied heavily upon his warriors. Images of them have been found, dressed as eagles, with their helmets sculpted as eagles' heads with open beaks. They seem almost super-human, which was no doubt the image that they wished to convey. When they marched on an expedition or an invasion, the warriors walked single-file. The scouts went ahead, followed by the priests carrying images of their gods. Their column

MOCTEZUMA II
Emperor Moctezuma II ruled the Aztec Empire with an almost godlike status. He was a religious man who thought the world would end if he did not offer human hearts to his gods.

would stretch for miles through the forests and mountain passes. The warriors' armor was made of quilted cotton so thick that it could stop an arrow. Their weapons included swords inset with sharp obsidian blades, javelins and spear-throwers, clubs and battle-sticks. When they went into battle, they uttered a series of ear-splitting shrieks and yells, which were accompanied by the sounds of whistles and conch shells. During the fighting itself, they sang and danced and, on most occasions, they managed to terrify or overwhelm their enemies. Victory was assured when the temple of the rival was seized or destroyed. This meant that the local god had surrendered, and their opponents saw no point in continuing the fight. These wars were fought over trade and land, but there is no doubt that they also had an underlying religious purpose.

War was seen as an aspect of Aztec religious duty. They had to keep fighting to maintain their identity as a chosen people. It was a civilization of nonstop war. The Aztec Empire was therefore continually expanding. Within a hundred years, the leaders had created an empire as large as any seen in Central America. But the empire was so large, and consisted of so many different types of people and terrain, that it was very difficult to control. It was made up of towns and city-states that had previously been independent. Certain territories

EAGLE AND JAGUAR WARRIORS
Noble soldiers who took four captives were entitled to join the elite eagle or jaguar (left) troops. They wore armor to resemble these sacred creatures and to show off their achievements.

were colonized, others were brought under Aztec supervision by means of marriage alliances or by appointing chieftains who would obey Aztec orders. But the Aztecs did not have enough resources to leave an army in occupation in every area they controlled—it has been estimated that there were some 400 local powers under Aztec control—and they did not use a system of governors. There was no centralized rule. Instead, they left in each town a tax-collector with a staff of officials, whose job it was to collect gifts known as tribute from the conquered people. Failure to provide these gifts resulted in instant reprisals and further warfare.

And tribute, of course, was the main reason for conquest. It poured into Tenochtitlán from all areas of the empire. There were cotton blankets and live birds, jewels and turtles, snakes and pots, wild animals and mats, feathers and wood. There were corn and beans, ants and bananas, bees and rats and roses, gold and slaves, incense and rubber balls, furniture and jade, salt and turkeys. Anything that any small region possessed or manufactured, it had to give. The produce and the wares came in daily, transported by canoes into the canals of Tenochtitlán or carried in by human bearers. And this is how the capital city of Tenochtitlán grew from a small marshy outpost into a city of some 300,000 people. By the early 16th century, it was the largest city in the world outside Asia.

CAPITAL GAINS
This is a copy of a page from the Aztec book the *Codex Mendoza*. It lists the names of towns paying tribute to Moctezuma's Tenochtitlán. The left side uses hieroglyphs to represent the towns, while the other symbols show the items each town had to deliver to the capital, such as beads and feathers.

INTO BATTLE
By law, every Aztec man had to serve military service in the emperor's army. Soldiers used obsidian-edged swords, as well as bows, slings, and spears, to fight in battle. They acted on behalf of the empire to crush any resistance. Soldiers carried different-colored shields according to their level in the army.

CHAPTER FOUR

Life *on the* lake

The Aztec city of Tenochtitlán was known as "the foundation of heaven." When the Spaniards first saw the city in 1519, they marveled. They thought it must be an enchanted city and asked themselves whether they were in some kind of dream.

TENOCHTITLÁN WAS A VAST CITY created on mud flats in the middle of a lake. There were several great causeways leading to it across the water, while the streets of the city itself were very straight and broad. The four main thoroughfares were aligned with the direction of the principal winds and, from a distance, the city would

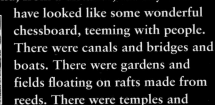

have looked like some wonderful chessboard, teeming with people. There were canals and bridges and boats. There were gardens and fields floating on rafts made from reeds. There were temples and palaces soaring in the mist, tall white towers rising above the white, flat-roofed and single-storied houses of the inhabitants. Among these dwellings rose painted pyramids. There were flowers and courtyards and markets and warehouses—the whole energy and activity of human life taking place on this island city.

◀ From a distance, Tenochtitlán seemed to float on the lake

CITY OF THE CACTUS
This picture represents Tenochtitlán's division into the four main sections of Atzacualco, Cuepopan, Moyotlan, and Teopan. Each area mirrored all the others. In the very center was a shrine to the Aztec god Huitzilopochtli, who was guardian of the city.

In one early map of Tenochtitlán, the ritual space in the center of the city is so enlarged that it takes up a third of the space of the city. This was, in fact, the reality of Tenochtitlán. The ritual center, with its temples and pyramids, was the sacred heart of the city, and it influenced every aspect of life. All roads led to this place of sacrifice and worship, which was dominated by the Great, or Double, Temple, built atop a huge pyramid. The city was organized into four quarters carved out by four avenues, which led from the gates of the ritual center. Each of these quarters had its own temple complex for the gods of that particular area. It is not surprising that the Aztecs believed that the gods had planned the city themselves.

Within each quarter there were the *calpulli*, or groups of houses united by family ties or trade. Each was a district, with its own temple, administered by the local leader, or *calpullec*. There was a district for market traders, for the makers of feather mosaics, for close family units, and so on. In all, there may have been as many as 70 such districts in the city. At a later date in the city's history, each *calpulli* also had a *telpochcalli*, or "youth house," a college with the general purpose of educating the young residents.

The city was governed and organized by state officials and clerks, who monitored every aspect of its activity. There was a system for gathering taxes from each household, and a system for organizing public labor. There were district priests as well as district leaders. The whole structure of society was rigidly controlled, from the lowest serf to the highest members of the ruling class. The warriors had their own place and role in life, and the common people had theirs. The merchants and the artisans had their position. There were slaves, too, some of whom had sold themselves in order to pay off debts.

You could tell if a person was a commoner or a member of the nobility by looking at the clothes he or she wore. While all men wore loincloths (strips of fabric wound around the waist and between the legs, with fabric hanging down front and back), some also wore cloaks. The quality of the cloth, and the patterns printed on it, were dictated by the wearer's position in society.

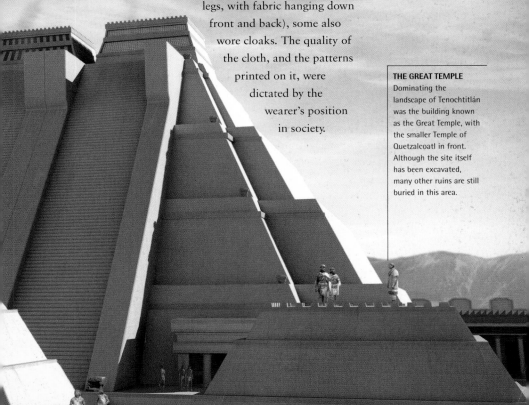

THE GREAT TEMPLE
Dominating the landscape of Tenochtitlán was the building known as the Great Temple, with the smaller Temple of Quetzalcoatl in front. Although the site itself has been excavated, many other ruins are still buried in this area.

Moctezuma decreed that only nobles were permitted to wear garments made of cotton. Commoners wore clothes made from the stiff, coarse fibers of the maguey plant. Even if a merchant became very wealthy, he would not be allowed to wear rich clothes because he was not a member of the nobility. If anyone wore something to which he or she was not entitled, punishment was severe.

There were strict rules that limited and controlled the citizens' lives from the very moment of their birth. As soon as a midwife had helped to deliver a baby, she was supposed to address a speech to the newborn. To the baby girls, she expounded upon the values of modesty and of domestic work, while to the baby boys she proclaimed the virtues of offering the blood of enemies to the sun. Throughout their childhood, children were trained to be dutiful and obedient, at the risk of being punished severely. One punishment involved hanging naughty children over a bowl of boiling chili peppers

Floating fields

On the island city of Tenochtitlán, land for growing crops was scarce. To overcome this problem, farmers constructed "floating" fields, which were known as *chinampas*. These did not actually float but were made out of fertile mud taken from the bottom of the lake and piled onto marshy areas to form rectangular plots. Each plot could be as long as 300 ft (90 m) and up to 30 ft (9 m) wide and was separated from its neighbor by a deep channel of water. These gardens supplied the city with flowers and vegetables. Farmers also cultivated some of the vast quantities of corn that were needed by the city. Families often lived on these plots to tend the crops and renew the soil when it looked less fertile.

Willow trees were planted along the edges to hold the soil together.

Farmers scooped soil from the lake bed and piled it into a plot.

Willow roots helped to bind the chinampa together.

Wooden stakes hammered into the ground prevented the soil from washing away.

where they were forced to breathe in the hot, spicy fumes. From a young age, children were taught the practical skills they would need in later life. Boys as young as four were encouraged to join their fathers on hunting trips, to help with catching fish and carrying out their everyday tasks. Girls helped their mothers with cooking, cleaning, weaving, and other jobs that Aztec women were expected to do. Between the ages of 10 and 20 (although these ages are disputed), both boys and girls would spend some time at school—perhaps the only example, at that time, of education being available to everyone in society, regardless of rank or wealth.

TEACHING WEAVING
Mothers taught their daughters to weave on a loom, using cotton or maguey fibers. The woven items were for their families and for payment of tribute and taxes.

There were two types of schools—the *telpochcalli*, which were for children from ordinary families, and the *calmecac*, where the children of the nobility were sent to study. Students at both types of schools were taught history and law, dance and song. The boys were trained to become warriors, and the girls were instructed in religious rites and practices, until it was time for marriage. At the *calmecac*, noble children were prepared for their future roles

CATCHING FISH
Fathers taught their sons to use huge nets and three-pointed spears to catch fish. Hooks were made from cactus thorns, shell, and bone. When boys reached 14 years old, they went fishing alone.

as priests, military leaders, or government officials. Life here was harsh, with students expected to fast, pray, and sacrifice their own blood by piercing their ears and legs with thorns. It was a very hard education, made more so by the stern discipline that was applied.

Yet out of this discipline and education emerged a code of what can be called Aztec ethics. Be moderate in all things; respect and obey your superiors; work hard; be just in all your dealings with your fellow men and women; exercise self-control; try to remain polite and grave in all your actions; be charitable toward the poor and to strangers; walk at a moderate pace; speak in a measured tone. There was a system of severe laws to maintain this social discipline.

SLAVES FOR SALE
The poorest Aztecs were slaves sold in the market. However, they did have rights—they were allowed to save money and buy land. Gamblers sometimes sold themselves into slavery in order to pay off debts.

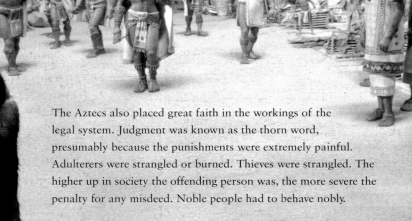

The Aztecs also placed great faith in the workings of the legal system. Judgment was known as the thorn word, presumably because the punishments were extremely painful. Adulterers were strangled or burned. Thieves were strangled. The higher up in society the offending person was, the more severe the penalty for any misdeed. Noble people had to behave nobly.

Life on the lake generally ran smoothly. There was a great market, which astonished the invading Spaniards with its orderliness and cleanliness. Each area of the market was methodically and carefully laid out. There was a place where the skins of jaguars were sold. The sellers of vegetables were in another spot, beside the sellers of herbs and the sellers of kidney beans. There were fruiterers and purveyors of cooked food. There were stalls for jugs and stalls for urns. There was an area for the sale of sandals and another for the sale of honey. There was a section where young dogs were sold for the cooking pot. There was an area for the sale of slaves, with poles tied across their shoulders to prevent them from escaping. (If they had escaped, where could they possibly have hidden in such a closely supervised city?)

BUSY MARKET
Although the market bustled with produce changing hands and people sharing news, it remained orderly. Market officials were on hand to resolve any disputes between traders and customers.

STAPLE DIET
Mesoamerican life centered around the planting, cultivating, and harvesting of crops, especially corn. Women ground dried corn kernels on a special grinding stone to create a coarse type of flour. This was used to make tortillas.

There were barber shops, as well as pharmacies and places to eat. All life and all forms of trade were here, engaged in the endless process of barter and exchange. There was no money in the modern sense. Aztec currency was cacao beans, cloaks, brightly colored feathers, and quills filled with gold. Anyone caught stealing, or selling stolen property, was instantly sentenced to death. We may assume that it was a particularly honest society. In the market itself there was no shouting or disorder. According to one observer, the sound was one of general humming or murmuring, like a vast swarm of worker bees.

The essential diet of the Aztecs was made up of the vegetables closest to hand and most easily cultivated—corn and beans, squash and chili peppers. But they also grew avocados and tomatoes, sweet potatoes and edible yucca (a type of cactus). In all, it is estimated that they raised almost 50 varieties of domestic

CHILI PEPPERS
Whether fresh or dried, hot chili peppers were popular. They were used as spices in all types of cooking.

plants, ranging from marigolds to papaya. They ate tortillas (filled flatbreads) flavored with a chili sauce, and tamales (stuffed corn husks) with beans. They also ate insects and salamanders as well as dogs and turkeys. They caught fish from the surrounding waters, but they also enjoyed tadpoles and water-flies. They ate popcorn and peanuts and chewed on a native gum known as chicle. They enjoyed a special type of hot chocolate drink, which could be flavored in a variety of ways. They smoked tobacco in pipes, and drank an alcoholic beverage made from the distilled sap of a special plant. Drunkenness, however, was punished by death.

Drinking water from mountain springs on the mainland was brought into the heart of the city by means of a great aqueduct, some 3 miles (5 km) in length. A second aqueduct was later constructed to meet the needs of the growing urban population. Water for washing was taken from the lake. The city was indeed very clean. A thousand men were employed to sweep and wash the streets each evening. You could walk barefoot almost anywhere in Tenochtitlán without dirtying your feet.

There was no transportation in the city except by boat or on the bent backs of human porters. There were no beasts of burden—the Aztecs, as we will see, were horrified when they first saw the horses of the Spaniards—and no wheeled vehicles. It is a curious fact that the Aztecs knew about wheels, and attached them to their toys, but made no use of them in their daily lives. The absence of animals large and strong enough to pull wheeled vehicles may partly account for this significant omission, but the wheel could have been useful to them in many other ways. It remains an ongoing puzzle to historians why the Aztecs seem to have ignored its possibilities.

But it is a mark of some great civilizing force that the original Aztecs—hunters and wayfarers, living in huts made of mud and reeds—should, within a relatively short space of time, construct such an elaborate and harmonious urban structure. It tells us much about the Aztecs themselves, particularly their energy and their burning sense of purpose.

TOYS ON WHEELS
Very young children stayed at home and played with toys. This pottery dog is an example of how the Aztecs used wheels for decorative purposes only. They never used wheels to help themselves get around.

TAMALES
A regular meal for the Aztecs was *tamales.* These were made from corn dough mixed with beans and chili peppers, wrapped in corn husks and steamed.

CHAPTER FIVE

Center
of sacrifice

The never-ending cycle of life was central to the Aztec view of the world. This was seen in their calendars, their festivals, and their sacrifice of human blood to keep the universe in order. To this end, the heart of the city became the ritual center of death.

ALL ROADS IN TENOCHTITLÁN led to the sacred center of the city—the place of worship and the place of sacrifice. This was where the Aztecs believed that all life began and ended—and it was certainly impressive. The whole area was paved, and enclosed by a wall known as the Snake Wall because it was decorated with huge serpent heads. Within the walls were many splendid buildings. There was a pyramid and temple devoted to Tezcatlipoca, Lord of the Smoking Mirror, the god of destiny and the favored patron of rulers. There was a temple to Quetzalcoatl, the Feathered Serpent, with its doors carved to resemble the open jaws of the serpent. There was a temple to the goddess known as Snake Woman. There was even a temple devoted to all the gods that the Aztecs had captured from rival cities. And there was, of course, a temple to the sun.

◀ Skull rack at the Great Temple, Tenochtitlán

Within the city center there was also a ball court where the somewhat macabre ritual game known as *tlachtli* was played. This court had a narrow playing area with sloping walls. It was a tough, and rough, sport and was taken very seriously by its players. And no wonder—the loser or losers were often sacrificed to the gods. The sacred center of Tenochtitlán also had areas for prayer and penance, where the priests would pierce their legs with thorns or use cords to rip their tongues. There were monasteries and religious schools, as well as "houses of the javelins" where weapons were collected and kept. There was a school for the court musicians and hostels for noble visitors.

And there were palaces. Each king created his own new palace, and tried to outdo his predecessors' palaces in size and luxury. The palace of Moctezuma II was extremely elaborate—a place of many courts and many rooms. There was a house of birds, containing examples of all the singing birds of the region, and gardens filled with the most fragrant flowers, as well as lakes and waterfalls. There were wooden cages in which live jaguars paced, and living quarters for singers and musicians. The courts of justice and halls of council, where the military and religious leaders of the Aztecs met in conference, were also in the palace. The public treasury was here, and the prison.

BALL GAME

The Aztecs played a variety of ball games. The most famous of these involved passing a hard rubber ball through a stone ring. The players used their hips to move the ball along.

Yet the royal palaces were not the central point of this vast ritual precinct. That honor was reserved for the Great, or Double, Temple built on top of a giant pyramid. This was the site of blood and sacrifice. Both temples had great pyramid-shaped roofs. The temple of the sun god was decorated with real human skulls, painted black and red, while the temple of the rain god was painted blue and white. By the temples lay the sacrificial stone where victims were taken. The pyramid on which the temples stood was the largest in the empire, with 114 steps rising to its summit. It was painted in white lime, dazzling the spectator in the bright sun. At its base was a great stone image of a goddess who had been beheaded and her body dismembered. The skull-rack, or *tzompantli*, where the decapitated heads of the sacrificial victims were displayed, was also here. This was the place where the sun, hungry for human blood, was renewed so that it could continue its course. This was the place where the gods were fed with the divine fire contained in a human heart and head. It was also the spot where all the forces of the spiritual world could be aligned in harmony, and where the pattern of the cosmos could be celebrated and renewed. Death was supposed to bring forth life.

BIGGER AND BETTER
The Great Temple was the center of the Aztec world, where human sacrifices and offerings to the gods took place. As each ruler tried to construct a more impressive temple than his predecessor, the pyramids were built one on top of another.

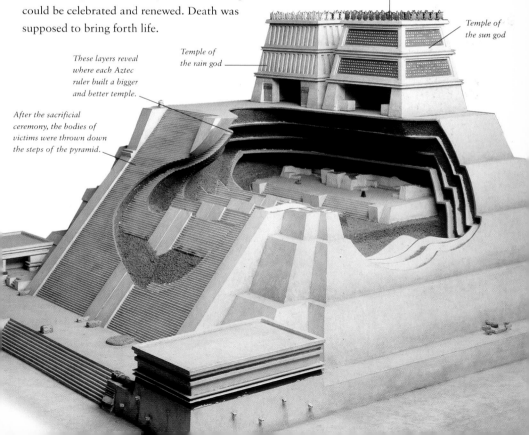

Temple of the sun god

Temple of the rain god

These layers reveal where each Aztec ruler built a bigger and better temple.

After the sacrificial ceremony, the bodies of victims were thrown down the steps of the pyramid.

Many of the victims of human sacrifice were captives of war. In fact, one of the most important aims of war was the capture of people to be sacrificed. When an Aztec captured one of his enemy, he would say, "Here is my well-beloved son," and the captive would reply, "Here is my revered father." Although they both knew that the captive would die when his heart was torn from his body, already there were ties of sympathy and fellow-feeling. For the Aztecs, sacrificial death was not an act of cruelty, but rather an act of regeneration.

Before the victims were dispatched to eternity, they were bathed and, on occasions, dressed in special costumes. They were taught chants and dances, as if they were about to attend a carnival. It seems that they were held in lines at the base of the pyramid until a priest led them in procession up the steps, which were already dyed scarlet with the blood of previous victims. At the summit, they were met by five priests, dressed in rich ceremonial clothes. The priests' faces and hands were painted black, and their foreheads were covered with discs of

SKULL MASK
This death's-head mask would have been worn during a religious ceremony. It was probably the skull of a sacrificial victim.

One of the priests makes the cut.

Sacrificial stone

Five priests hold the person down.

Heart of the matter

People in the Aztec world believed that, just as the gods sacrificed themselves during the creation of the sun and moon, they had to do the same. They took no joy from killing but felt it was necessary to feed the gods to keep the cosmic order and ensure the continuity of life. Most sacrifices were performed in honor of the sun, rain, and earth gods. The victims were generally prisoners taken in time of war.

Removing the heart
Five priests, sometimes with their faces smeared in different colors, held the victim by the arms and legs. The heart was plucked from the victim and placed in a special holder.

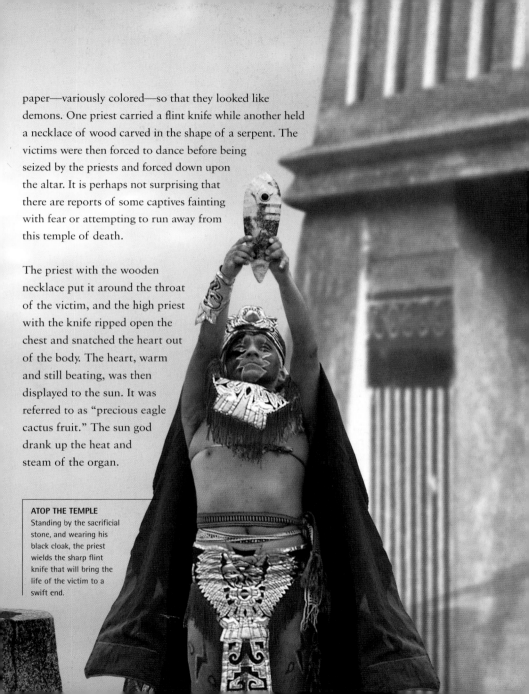

paper—variously colored—so that they looked like
demons. One priest carried a flint knife while another held
a necklace of wood carved in the shape of a serpent. The
victims were then forced to dance before being
seized by the priests and forced down upon
the altar. It is perhaps not surprising that
there are reports of some captives fainting
with fear or attempting to run away from
this temple of death.

The priest with the wooden
necklace put it around the throat
of the victim, and the high priest
with the knife ripped open the
chest and snatched the heart out
of the body. The heart, warm
and still beating, was then
displayed to the sun. It was
referred to as "precious eagle
cactus fruit." The sun god
drank up the heat and
steam of the organ.

ATOP THE TEMPLE
Standing by the sacrificial
stone, and wearing his
black cloak, the priest
wields the sharp flint
knife that will bring the
life of the victim to a
swift end.

The heart was then placed in a sacred vessel as an offering to the gods. The blood of those who had been sacrificed was used to coat the walls and shrines and statues of the Great Temple. The blood was also fed to the images of the gods. After the heart had been removed, the lifeless body was thrown down the steps of the pyramid, passing those who were being led to the same death. At the bottom of the pyramid the corpse was flayed, and the skull placed on the *tzompantli*. The remains were then claimed by those who had originally captured the prisoner. They took the body and ate it. The flesh was cooked with corn.

SACRIFICIAL KNIVES
Stone and flint knives were used to kill sacrificial victims. Shells and stone were added to the handles and blades to symbolize the faces of the gods for whom the hearts were intended.

But it was not only men captured in war who were sacrificed. There were regular sacrifices of women and children. Women were painted in bright colors and adorned with golden bells. They danced and sang all night before being led to their deaths. Children were seen as ideal victims for sacrifice, possibly because they were pure and innocent and had not been alive for very long, which meant that they were closer to the gods. Children were sacrificed to the rain god, Tlaloc, by being thrown into Lake Texcoco. Their tears were thought to be a very good sign—the more they cried, the more it would rain.

It is definitely not pleasant to record these details, but it is important to realize that this had become a culture obsessed with death. It was also a culture built upon insecurity and worry. The Aztecs believed that at the end of every cycle of 52 years, the universe might come to an end. The sun was unstable and might not rise again. They also believed that the gods needed blood in order to continue their work. Offering up the heart was not just a ritual, it was essential. If they stopped the practice of human sacrifice, the universe would come to an end.

The sun needed to drink up blood before it could continue its journey through the heavens.

There must be some suspicion, however, that the Aztec leaders also used mass sacrifice as a way of controlling their people and their empire. The system rewarded the soldiers who captured prisoners, and merchants who bought slaves for sacrifice, as well as those who offered up their own slaves. It was a society of savage spectacle, designed to awe and to terrify. Yet it was a society filled with contradictions. When the priests sacrificed small children, it is reported that they moaned and wept together with their captives. There was no pleasure taken in the ritual—it was seen as a matter of stern necessity. It was a culture that loved flowers and poetry and the sweet sound of birds, but also one engaged in acts of mass extermination. It was a very clean city, washed every evening, but at its heart was a bloody slaughterhouse.

BODY-THROWING
This scene shows what happened to the dead body. After it was thrown down the stairs, the corpse was flayed and the remains were given to whoever had first captured the victim. The warrior would then practice cannibalism with what was left.

Another bloody practice was the ritual of self-mutilation and self-laceration. The Aztecs did this to produce the blood that was needed to move the heavens and the earth. They cut parts of their body with thorns, or sharpened tools, or the spines of fish, and allowed the blood to flow or drip onto pieces of paper, which were then burned as a sacrifice. They cut their tongue, or their genitals, or their leg, to produce the "precious water."

WARRING AZTECS
These scenes show warriors taking captives. The Flower Wars were small, prearranged battles aimed at capturing victims to offer as future sacrifices. The more captives a warrior took, the more elaborate his costume became.

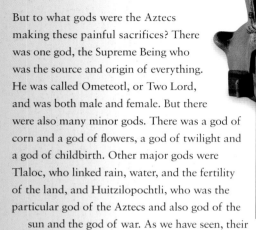

EARTH GODDESS
Coatlicue (Serpent Skirt) was the earth goddess and the mother of the sun god and the god of war, Huitzilopochtli. She had already given birth to the moon and stars when she gave birth to the god of the sun. This statue shows her skirt made of serpents.

But to what gods were the Aztecs making these painful sacrifices? There was one god, the Supreme Being who was the source and origin of everything. He was called Ometeotl, or Two Lord, and was both male and female. But there were also many minor gods. There was a god of corn and a god of flowers, a god of twilight and a god of childbirth. Other major gods were Tlaloc, who linked rain, water, and the fertility of the land, and Huitzilopochtli, who was the particular god of the Aztecs and also god of the sun and the god of war. As we have seen, their temples sat atop the Great Pyramid. And, of course, there was the Feathered Serpent, Quetzalcoatl, whose cult throughout Mesoamerica has been described in an earlier chapter.

THE MASK OF TLALOC
The goggle-eyed rain god Tlaloc was also associated with agricultural fertility. He was widely worshiped, and many Mesoamerican sculptures depict his face.

The priests who worshiped and sacrificed to these deities lived in special colleges and abstained from contact with women. They wore black robes and hoods. Their cloaks were embroidered with images of skulls and human bones. Their fingernails were very long and their waist-length hair was clotted with human blood. Their limbs and tongue—and other more private parts of their bodies—were pierced and scarred by the practice of self-mutilation. They must have been objects of awe and terror among the population. But they were also honored as good and wise men, who could read the patterns of the night sky and interpret dreams or visions. They administered the temples and supervised the lands belonging to the temples.

At the core of their faith, the Aztecs believed that there had been five ages of the world, or five Suns, and that they were living in the fifth age. The first period was Four Jaguar, when giants

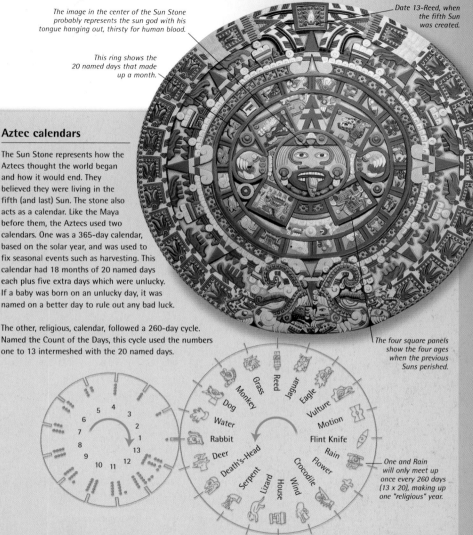

The image in the center of the Sun Stone probably represents the sun god with his tongue hanging out, thirsty for human blood.

Date 13-Reed, when the fifth Sun was created.

This ring shows the 20 named days that made up a month.

The four square panels show the four ages when the previous Suns perished.

One and Rain will only meet up once every 260 days (13 x 20), making up one "religious" year.

Aztec calendars

The Sun Stone represents how the Aztecs thought the world began and how it would end. They believed they were living in the fifth (and last) Sun. The stone also acts as a calendar. Like the Maya before them, the Aztecs used two calendars. One was a 365-day calendar, based on the solar year, and was used to fix seasonal events such as harvesting. This calendar had 18 months of 20 named days each plus five extra days which were unlucky. If a baby was born on an unlucky day, it was named on a better day to rule out any bad luck.

The other, religious, calendar, followed a 260-day cycle. Named the Count of the Days, this cycle used the numbers one to 13 intermeshed with the 20 named days.

The religious calendar

Each day had a name and number, which both changed daily. This is shown here by representing each as separate wheels in a cog. The numbers ran from one to 13, and the names repeated every 20 days. So if today was One-Rabbit, tomorrow would be Two-Water and the day after would be Three-Dog. After 13 days, the new "week" would begin with One-Crocodile, then Two-Wind, and so on. By the end of the "year" (260 days), each of the 20 days would have had a turn at being the "One" day.

roamed the earth. This period ended when the jaguars ate the giants. The second era was Four Wind. This era was destroyed by great whirlwinds, and the inhabitants of the earth were turned into monkeys. The third period, Four Rain, ended in a rain of fire and the people were transformed into birds. The fourth era, Four Water, concluded in floods, when the people became fish. The present, fifth, era, known as Four Movement, was the one in which men and women were created. It was prophesied that it would end in earthquakes and universal famine. So there was no progress in the Aztec world, only an endless cycle of creation and destruction.

FESTIVE DAYS
Farmers grew flowers, as well as corn, on their floating fields. These were used in Aztec festivals throughout the year.

SMOKING MOUNTAIN
From Tenochtitlán, the impressive volcano Popocatepetl ("smoking mountain") was visible. Some Aztec festivals honored the landscape.

There were a number of rituals and festivals specifically intended to ward off that day of death and destruction, and to maintain the sun on its steady course. There were some 18 annual festivities, one for each of the 18 months in the Aztec year. No festivities were held on the five days of the year that were considered unlucky and were known as "useless days." The year's festivals began with the Ending of the Water and the Raising of the Trees, in which children were sacrificed to the rain god, sacrificed to the god of fire, and corn was toasted. During this festival children were pulled by the neck, to help them grow. Between these two rituals were others of a more gentle kind. In one of them, flowers and ears of corn were carried by young women to the temple. In many others, the king or *tlatoani* danced in front of his people. There was a festival in which young men climbed poles, and another in which the mountains were honored. In one festival, the priests and young warriors went into battle against each other armed with reeds. If a priest was captured, he was rubbed all over with a kind of stinging nettle. In another month, young women were painted in bright colors, and were allowed to mock any young men they encountered.

There were also some less happy celebrations. In the festival known as the Beautiful Man, the most handsome male captive was chosen as the embodiment of the god Tezcatlipoca, the god of destiny. The victim lived in the greatest luxury and comfort for a year. He was dressed in eagle feathers and flowers, and his body was ornamented with gold. He walked through the streets of Tenochtitlan, and the people treated him as if he were a living god. He spoke graciously to everyone, and played for them on the flute or whistle. Twenty days before his sacrifice he was given four young women as his wives. They all danced together in front of the people as a symbol of their harmony. On the day of his death, he was taken by boat to a temple outside the city. As he climbed the steps of this temple, he broke his whistles and his flutes. When he arrived at the summit, he was taken by the

THE BEAUTIFUL MAN
A handsome male, known as the Beautiful Man, was chosen as the earthly representative of the god of destiny. He was forced to dance before he was killed.

THE PLEIADES
This star cluster has long been visible in the night sky. Crucial to the New Fire Ceremony, the Pleiades consists of six main stars visible to the naked eye and 500 other faint stars.

priests and quickly slaughtered, his heart ripped out and his head cut off. So ended the strange history of the Beautiful Man.

The most spectacular festival of all, however, occurred only once every 52 years, when the Aztecs believed that it could be the end of time—the period in which the fifth Sun might be extinguished. This, then, was the most significant and dangerous day in Aztec history. The festival was known as the Binding of the Years, and a bundle of 52 reeds was symbolically collected together as an act of commemoration. The day was marked by what was known as the New Fire Ceremony. As night fell, all the fires and lights of Tenochtitlán and the other Aztec communities were put out, so that the people could watch the movement of the night sky.

BUNDLE OF 52 REEDS
Priests recorded time by saving a reed for each year that passed. At the end of 52 years, when the Aztecs thought the world might end, the reeds were burned at a special ceremony. This carving shows the 52 reeds.

A procession of priests advanced from the city to an ancient shrine known as the Thorn Tree Place. It was on the summit of a hill, called the Hill of the Star, that overlooked Lake Texcoco, and could be seen from far away. A priest made a fire on the chest of the warrior to be sacrificed, then carried the fire to a great bonfire of wood. At the precise moment when a group of stars known as the Pleiades crossed the meridian (an imaginary circle that runs from north to south around the heavens and earth), the victim's heart was ripped out and thrown into this fire. A little while later, at midnight, the whole body was thrown into the fire. As the fire blazed, a great cry of joy and relief came from the land of the Aztecs. The flames leaped up, and a group of messengers lit their torches from them. Like Olympic runners, they carried the sacred fire to the various cities and towns of the region. The fires were given to each neighborhood, and some of the inhabitants would throw themselves upon the flames. Their burns were seen as a symbol of renewal. It was the beginning of time. A new cycle of life had begun.

A NEW YEAR BEGINS

The New Fire Ceremony occurred once every 52 years. On this special night, priests and a warrior victim chosen by the king walked to the top of the Hill of the Star. A sacred fire was lit and the Aztecs celebrated a new beginning.

CHAPTER SIX

Rise and fall
of the Aztecs

The Aztecs, who believed that the gods existed in every living thing, wanted to glorify the natural world with their art and music. There was much to celebrate. On the horizon, however, invaders were on the way, and this unique era was to end in violence.

THE AZTEC WORLD MAY HAVE been obsessed with death and sacrifice, yet out of this darkness there emerged art and poetry, song and dance. There were many types of Aztec artists. There were the feather artists who used brilliant quetzal and hummingbird feathers mixed with eagle down to create impressive patterns. They placed their work on reed frames or pasted them onto cloth or paper. There were painters of frescoes and murals as well as sculptors and stonemasons, potters, and smiths working in precious metals. The painters used vivid colors to rival the yellow brilliance of the parrot or the green depths of jade stone. The Aztecs loved radiance and brightness, living as they did in a forest world that was filled with vibrant color. That is why they loved the appearance and scent of flowers—much of their poetry is devoted to the blossoms that surrounded them.

◀ Feather shield, probably owned by Moctezuma

The main concern
of the artists, however,
lay in finding a way to express
the sacred world that lay within the
natural world. They believed that the gods
existed inside every living thing—whether it was a
rabbit, a cob of corn, or a young maiden. The Aztecs were
great carvers of stone, too, because they believed that in creating
monumental sculptures or tiny figurines, they were creating prayers
in stone. It is common to see open mouths and clenched fists in their
sculptures of the human form because these signify the presence of a
god. Aztec sculpture is, in fact, more realistic than the heads of the
Olmecs or the warrior images of the Toltecs. There are stone images of
old men, goddesses, and female nudes. There are images of the cactus
and the pumpkin as well as little figures of rabbits and dogs, with
surprisingly human expressions. There are images of insects, of fish, of
lizards, and of rattlesnakes. The Aztecs glorified all the creatures of the
world, because they knew them to be holy.

In their workshops, the smiths created art in gold and other precious
metals. They made elaborate items of jewelry for the warriors and the
leading families. They fashioned rings and pendants, earrings and
rattles. These precious objects were also considered to be sacred,

GRAND DESIGNS
Many Aztec gods were
shown wearing elaborate
headdresses, and skilled
craftworkers often copied
these for their own
warriors. The rank of an
Aztec warrior was shown
by the grandeur of his
headdress and feather suit.

GOLD LIP ORNAMENTS
The lip plug, also known as a labret, was worn through a hole beneath the lower lip. Made from gold or jade, or a mixture of both, they were only worn by members of the elite.

MASK FOR THE DEAD
Masks were decorated with elaborate carvings, stunning mosaics, or precious stones. They covered the faces of the dead for burial or were worn during festivals.

because they were filled with the grandeur of the spirits and gods who lived inside these metals, bright as the sun. In fact, paintings show that when the Spaniards arrived, the Aztecs sent them a gold wheel measuring some 6½ ft (2 m) in diameter, as well as shields of pearl, a necklace bearing almost 200 emeralds and small gold bells, a helmet of gold, and various creatures fashioned out of gold. To the invaders, it seemed that they had reached a land of priceless treasures.

The Aztecs also created other ornaments out of gold. They made lip plugs—symbols of status—which were placed in a hole made through the lower lip. They made ornaments for the nose out of jewels or precious metals. Feather artists created fans, shields, and elaborate headdresses, and other artists crafted masks that were worn during the various festivals and celebrations. If you hid your face behind a mask, then you could impersonate—or you could become—an eagle or a jaguar. There are masks made of greenstone and of gold, of jade and of obsidian.

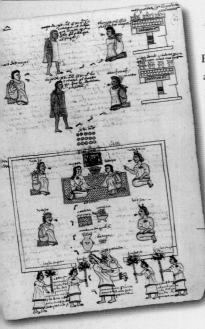

But the Aztecs were not only artists. They were also poets and storytellers. The range of Aztec literature was vast. It included works of law and medicine, of history and mythology as well as lyric (songlike) poems and epic (long) poems, songs, and rituals. The language of the Aztecs is known as Nahuatl, and it is a miracle of the civilization that it is still spoken in central Mexico today. The written language of the Aztecs took the form of glyphs. These are marks or symbols that can represent images or ideas. For example, war was represented by a shield and a club, while speech was shown by a scroll coming from the mouth of the person speaking. The idea of moving in a certain direction or a sequence of events would be shown by a series of footprints.

WEDDING DAY
This page from the *Codex Mendoza* shows a wedding ceremony. The couple in the center are shown with knotted cloaks, representing the bond of marriage.

Words and Numbers

The Aztecs always kept records. Their script used pictures and glyphs (symbols) to represent words. This system worked very well for objects that could be shown in a drawing, but more complex ideas and feelings could not be documented.

Footprints on this glyph suggest a journey.

Speech is represented by a scroll coming from the mouth.

The word conquest is represented by a burning temple.

Written records
The symbols used were not placed in a sentence order as we have in books today, but were placed in the form of a broader picture or a scene of glyphs. Since letters were not used to represent the sounds of speech, writing was never intended to be a total record. A priest, for example, could memorize his people's history, but the codex would remind him of the details.

The symbol for the number 1 was a dot or a finger.

A flag stood for the number 20.

This plant symbol stood for 400.

The symbol for 8,000 was a sack of cacao beans.

The flag indicates 20 of this unidentified item.

This means 400 blankets.

This means 8,000 feathers.

Counting
The Aztecs counted in multiples of 20. This worked as follows: 1, 20, 400 (20 x 20), and 8,000 (20 x 20 x 20). They showed the numbers in between by repeating each symbol up to 19 times. For example, if they wanted to indicate the number 180, they would show 20 (the flag) nine times.

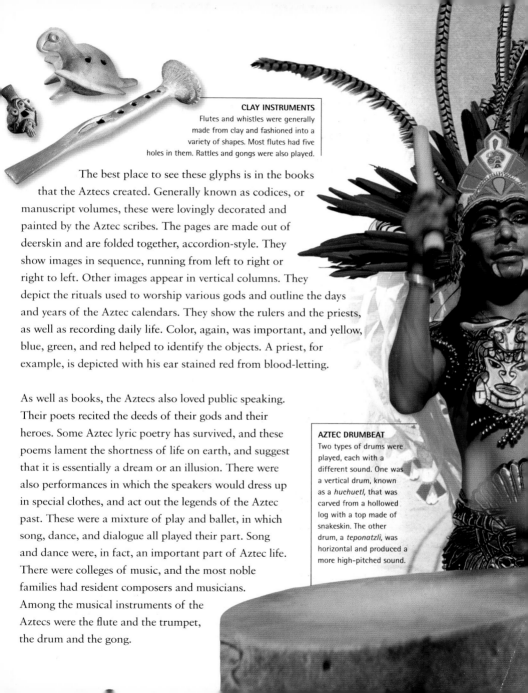

Flutes and whistles were generally made from clay and fashioned into a variety of shapes. Most flutes had five holes in them. Rattles and gongs were also played.

The best place to see these glyphs is in the books that the Aztecs created. Generally known as codices, or manuscript volumes, these were lovingly decorated and painted by the Aztec scribes. The pages are made out of deerskin and are folded together, accordion-style. They show images in sequence, running from left to right or right to left. Other images appear in vertical columns. They depict the rituals used to worship various gods and outline the days and years of the Aztec calendars. They show the rulers and the priests, as well as recording daily life. Color, again, was important, and yellow, blue, green, and red helped to identify the objects. A priest, for example, is depicted with his ear stained red from blood-letting.

As well as books, the Aztecs also loved public speaking. Their poets recited the deeds of their gods and their heroes. Some Aztec lyric poetry has survived, and these poems lament the shortness of life on earth, and suggest that it is essentially a dream or an illusion. There were also performances in which the speakers would dress up in special clothes, and act out the legends of the Aztec past. These were a mixture of play and ballet, in which song, dance, and dialogue all played their part. Song and dance were, in fact, an important part of Aztec life. There were colleges of music, and the most noble families had resident composers and musicians. Among the musical instruments of the Aztecs were the flute and the trumpet, the drum and the gong.

AZTEC DRUMBEAT
Two types of drums were played, each with a different sound. One was a vertical drum, known as a *huehuetl*, that was carved from a hollowed log with a top made of snakeskin. The other drum, a *teponatzli*, was horizontal and produced a more high-pitched sound.

And so the Aztec Empire flourished until the arrival of the Spaniards, led by Hernán Cortés, a religious and ambitious man with the twin aims of converting the local people to Christianity and winning fame and fortune for himself. Cortés arrived on the east coast of Mexico in 1519, in a Spanish fleet that was described by Aztec lookouts as a "mountain floating upon the water." At first, the ruler Moctezuma II believed that Cortés' arrival marked the return of the god Quetzalcoatl, the Feathered Serpent, who, according to legend, had sailed away into the east in ancient times. Moctezuma's welcome was warm. He offered the Spaniards great treasures, but this only served to fuel the invaders' determination and greed. The Spaniards left some sweet biscuits on the beach. These were collected with great respect by the Aztecs and, on Moctezuma's orders, they were covered with sacred cloths and taken in procession to the temple of the Feathered Serpent in Tula.

MOCTEZUMA'S HEADDRESS
This headdress was made from the feathers of the quetzal bird and the blue cotinga. It was part of the booty taken from the Aztecs and sent back to Spain by Cortés.

But this mood of worship could not have lasted for very long. Cortés' small army of adventurers and shabby gentlemen began their march toward the center of the Aztec Empire across the mountains and plateaus of the region. As they marched inland, they defeated the independent tribe of the Tlaxcalans, who then joined forces with them against their old enemy, the Aztecs. Then Cortés negotiated a further alliance with the Tepanecs, who had also long been hostile to Aztec domination. The Aztec Empire was beginning to disintegrate.

Disturbed by the success of these alien men, Moctezuma tried to placate them with elaborate gifts as they approached his kingdom. It is reported that captives were sent to them, with instructions that they should be killed and their blood drunk. The Aztec ruler sent them food, but that, too, was sprinkled with human blood.

Eventually, realizing that their advance could not be stopped, Moctezuma agreed to meet Cortés and his men outside his capital city of Tenochtitlán. The Aztec leader was carried out on his litter, dressed in all his glory. Cortés went to embrace him, but was stopped by the nobles, who refused to allow their ruler to be touched. Nonetheless, for the first time two great civilizations, parted by many thousands of years of separate development, met. There was a ritual exchange of gifts, and Moctezuma invited the Spaniards to one of the royal palaces in the center of the city.

Once inside the city, Cortés realized that he had to act quickly before he was overwhelmed by Aztec warriors. And so, using the excuse of a meeting with the king, Cortés and his men seized Moctezuma and declared him a prisoner. The shock to the Aztecs must have been profound. They were not used to secrecy or lies of any kind. And they could never have imagined that their supreme ruler—whose face could not be looked upon and whose body could not be touched— would be taken and held hostage. But that is what happened.

Over the next few months, Moctezuma remained under the control of the Spaniards. They permitted him to continue to rule his kingdom, but he was forced to allow the Spaniards to do more or less as they pleased within the city. This angered the people and nobles of Tenochtitlán, who grew increasingly restless. The situation was made infinitely worse when, in the temporary absence of Cortés, thousands

SPANISH FLEET
When the Spanish ships arrived on the coast, they were carrying 530 fighting men, 16 horses, 14 cannons, and hunting dogs. When the Aztecs first saw the billowing sails of these floating monsters, they thought it was their god, Quetzalcoatl, returning from the East.

of Aztec nobles, who had been participating in a ritual ceremony, were massacred by the Spaniards. Moctezuma tried to keep order among his people, but he had lost their respect. He was killed by unknown assailants—some say that he died as a result of stoning by his own enraged subjects, others that he was murdered by the Spaniards. Whatever the truth of the matter, the last true emperor of the Aztecs was dead.

SPANISH ARMS
While the Aztec army wore only padded cotton clothes, the Spanish were protected by steel armor. The Spanish also had the firepower of muskets and cannons to defend themselves from the weapons of their enemies.

New leaders swiftly emerged and fought a pitched battle against the Spaniards within the city. The Spaniards succeeded in overcoming their attackers, but, aware of their dangerous situation in the heart of an enemy capital, they fled by night. When the Spaniards returned nearly a year later, they came with a huge army of Aztec-hating allies. This time, the forces were more evenly matched—perhaps a quarter of a million men on each side. Cortés and his allies laid siege to Tenochtitlán and, after nearly four months, it fell on August 15, 1521. The Aztec Empire had come to an end. How was it that a force consisting initially of 530 men effectively destroyed an empire of perhaps as many as 11 million people? In one sense, there was no real competition. The Spaniards had far better weapons—

CITY DESTROYED
The Aztecs fought hard to defend their city. But as the bloody fighting continued, the lake began to turn red and the corpses piled up. The city of Tenochtitlán was completely destroyed.

cannons, muskets, swords, and metal armor—which gave
them the edge over the Aztec warriors. The Spaniards also
had horses, an animal unknown in Mesoamerica. At first
the Aztecs thought the horse and rider were separate parts
of the same creature, half-man and half-animal. Yet they
managed, in time, to overcome their fear of this strange
beast. What they could not overcome was the range of
European diseases that the invaders brought with them,
which up to this point were unknown in the region. When
Cortés made his final assault on Tenochtitlán, he was
fighting a people who had been decimated by an outbreak
of smallpox. Together with the support of his allies, it is no
wonder that he defeated the remaining Aztecs.

And so the Aztec resistance collapsed. Their temples were
destroyed, their idols burned or hacked to pieces, their
cities burned to the ground. Like the Olmecs and the
Toltecs before them, their civilization died in a cataclysm
of violence. It is one of the strangest cultures ever created
upon the earth, but its enduring legend has ensured that it
also remains one of the most fascinating.

The spread of disease

Although the Aztecs
were familiar with
illness, there was
little their healers
could do to stop
the spread of disease
brought by the
invading Europeans.

The virus that
causes smallpox

It is believed that a
Spanish soldier fell ill with smallpox in
1520 and by the following year, half of
Mexico's native population was dead.
They had no natural resistance to this
contagious and fatal disease. The name
"smallpox" is derived from the Latin word
for "spotted" and referred to the raised
lumps that spread over the faces and
bodies of sufferers.

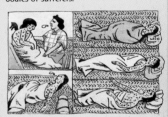

Victims of smallpox
This scene from one of the Aztec books, the
Codex Florentino, shows the devastating
effects of smallpox. Although Aztec healers
knew of more than 1,000 plants used for
medicinal purposes, they were of no help
against the symptoms of smallpox.

CHAPTER SEVEN

Mystery
of the Maya

Great ruined cities, evidence of a unique system of writing, and large blocks of elaborately carved stone lay hidden for centuries in the tropical forests. But the mystery of the Maya is now revealed to be the history of a unique and powerful civilization.

AFTER THE COLLAPSE of the Aztec Empire in 1521, the Spaniards, led by Cortés, moved eastward through Mesoamerica in their quest for more converts, more gold, and more glory. They came to a region called the Yucatán, where they encountered scattered communities of people who proved very difficult to subdue. These were the

Maya, the descendants of a people who had once formed an advanced civilization made up of numerous independent city-states linked by shared beliefs and a sophisticated network of trade routes. As Cortés and his men journeyed through the region, they found themselves caught among forests and lagoons, rivers and mountains, which seemed impossible to pass. It took them 16 years to overcome the Maya in the central Yucatán, and it was left to future generations of Spaniards to conquer the more remote Maya outposts some 150 years later.

◀ The remains of Tikal rise above the forests of Guatemala

Apart from some letters written home by the Spaniards, little more was heard about the Maya until the 19th century, when American and European explorers penetrated the tropical forests in search of the pyramids and temples of which they had read. They found great ruined cities, their turrets white and gleaming above the trees, and ancient limestone roads running from city to city. They found evidence of a unique writing system, and a series of symbols made up of bars and dots. They found great blocks of stone, known as stelae, covered with symbols and hieroglyphs. Some of these stelae had been uprooted by giant trees and lay shattered on the forest floor; others remained standing as witness to once-great rulers. They found statues of gods, shrouded by groves of silent trees. One archaeologist described the sites as places "of romance and wonder." These were cities of unknown origin and mysterious decay.

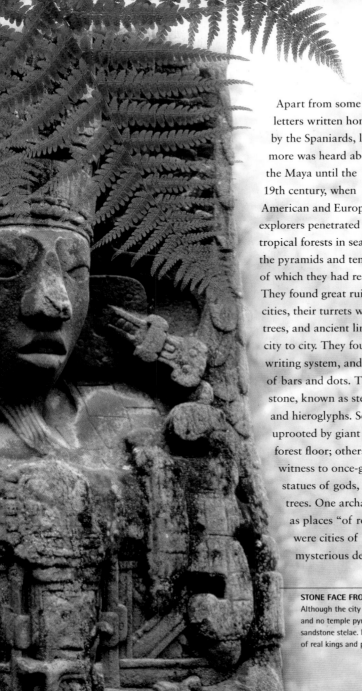

STONE FACE FROM QUIRIGUÁ

Although the city of Quiriguá has only a few stone ruins and no temple pyramids, the site is renowned for its huge sandstone stelae. Maya glyphic inscriptions and the faces of real kings and priests were carved into the stone.

MAJOR MAYA CITIES
This map locates some of the main Maya cities—
from the early settlement at Cuello to the last
powerful cities of Chichén Itzá and Mayapan.
Many cities were linked by giant causeways.

Chichén Itzá
Mayapan ■
Coba
Uxmal ■
Tulum ■
■ Labna

**Yucatán
Peninsula**

Gulf of Mexico

Xicalango ■

Becán ■
Calakmul ■
El Mirador ■
Cuello ■
Nakbé ■
Uaxactún ■

Caribbean Sea

Palenque ■

Tikal ■

■ Yaxchilán
■ Bonampak

PACIFIC OCEAN

■ Quiriguá
■ Copán

■ Kaminaljuyu

In place of mystery, many theories have been put forward. The Maya were the ten lost tribes of Israel, creating a new biblical civilization in the heart of the jungle. They were Egyptians who, having left their native soil, raised great pyramids under a strange sky. They were the survivors of the legendary underwater kingdom of Atlantis, recreating submerged palaces and temples on dry land. They came from outer space, their deformed heads proving them to be of alien origin. In truth, the people who would go on to build a great civilization first came into the region as hunters and gatherers. Some of their stone tools have been found, together with animal bones bearing the cut marks made by these tools. In the course of thousands of years, these ancestors of the Maya settled down. They lived in hamlets of ten or twelve huts and began to cultivate the corn and squash, beans and peppers, which remain part of the Maya diet today.

The land where the Maya lived covered the area that now makes up parts of Mexico, most notably the Yucatán and Campeche, and modern Belize, Guatemala, and the western regions of El Salvador and Honduras. The whole area lies in the tropics, but it is made up of very different geographic

Head-Binding

It was fashionable for Maya infants to have their heads reshaped. This was usually done by binding their heads tightly to boards. Over time, the skulls became the desired shape. This shape can be seen in many Maya and Olmec carvings.

The Maya used wooden boards to reshape the child's head.

The pressure from the boards changed the skull permanently.

EARLY POTTERY
The Maya were skilled at clay modeling. Cooking pots were made by pressing clay into molds. These were often decorated and engraved, like this bowl.

areas, ranging from flat limestone plateaus to tropical jungles and ranges of volcanic mountains. There are forests of cedar and mahogany and palms, but there are also great plains of grass known as savanna. There are lakes and rivers, streams and swamps, but there are also arid valleys and ravines. Large areas of the Yucatán have practically no rivers or streams, and water was collected from natural wells known as cenotes. As we will discover, these cenotes were considered sacred by the Maya.

In these surroundings, the Maya began to grow and prosper. By 1800 BCE, the hamlets of the first farming communities had become villages where people grew corn and a plant called manioc, which had a starchy root from which they made a type of flour. They still engaged in hunting and gathering, but they also tried to change the natural world around them. They cleared some of the forest land by means of a technique called "slash and burn." As its name suggests, the farmers would cut down and burn the vegetation of a certain area, and then plant crops in the ashes before the seasonal rains began. The Maya's later obsession with time and the calendar may have arisen from their need to make sure that the corn crop was planted at exactly the right time of the year for the best chance of a good harvest. These early villagers also learned how to manufacture simple pottery. From these modest beginnings rose a unique civilization.

An early indication of that civilization comes from a village in northern Belize called Cuello, which emerged

RAIN GOD CHAC
The god of rain was held in such esteem that some Maya buildings were covered with his masks. Chac can be recognized here by his protruding teeth.

between 1000 and 700 BCE. Archaeologists have found evidence of a
building constructed on a raised round platform with a fire pit in
front of it, which suggests that rituals were performed here. Cuello
was probably only one of many such settlements with ritual spaces.
As villages grew into small towns, they attracted other people from
the surrounding area. It also seems likely that a group of aristocratic
leaders emerged during this period. These elite groups were probably
made up of priests or warriors, or a combination of the two. It
should be remembered that this early period of Maya development

DEEP UNDERGROUND
During droughts, children
were thrown into the deep
wells, or *cenotes*, as a
means of pleading with
the rain god Chac to end
the drought. The Maya
also threw offerings into
the well, which they
believed to be sacred.

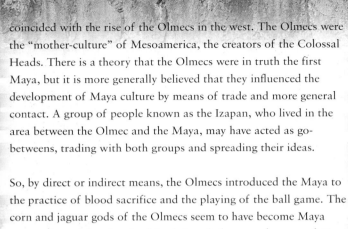

coincided with the rise of the Olmecs in the west. The Olmecs were the "mother-culture" of Mesoamerica, the creators of the Colossal Heads. There is a theory that the Olmecs were in truth the first Maya, but it is more generally believed that they influenced the development of Maya culture by means of trade and more general contact. A group of people known as the Izapan, who lived in the area between the Olmec and the Maya, may have acted as go-betweens, trading with both groups and spreading their ideas.

So, by direct or indirect means, the Olmecs introduced the Maya to the practice of blood sacrifice and the playing of the ball game. The corn and jaguar gods of the Olmecs seem to have become Maya gods, too. But despite this obvious link, many features of Maya culture were unique to them. Only they built great causeways of stone between their temples. They created a new, elaborate form of art in which every single available space on a work was covered in images, and every single image had a carefully defined meaning. They invented a type of arch, built using a system of overlapping stones, which was known as corbeling. And they invented a new system for recording time.

As the Olmecs declined, so the Maya rose. Cities grew from the small towns of the earlier Maya world. These cities were largely administrative and ceremonial centers, and their populations were not large. Nonetheless, an intensive program of agriculture was needed to feed their inhabitants. Canals and reservoirs had to be built to provide water. The cities were filled with public architecture and ceremonial precincts. There were temples with thatched roofs as well as stone stairways and plaster pavements, generally painted red.

It was a time when power, military or religious, was being celebrated. It was a time of leaders and of a society divided into groups with

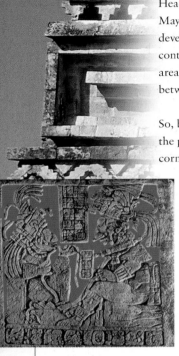

BLOODLETTING RELIEF
In this relief, the ruler Shield Jaguar watches as his wife, Lady Xoc, performs a blood sacrifice by drawing a rope of thorns through her tongue. The blood would have been offered to the gods.

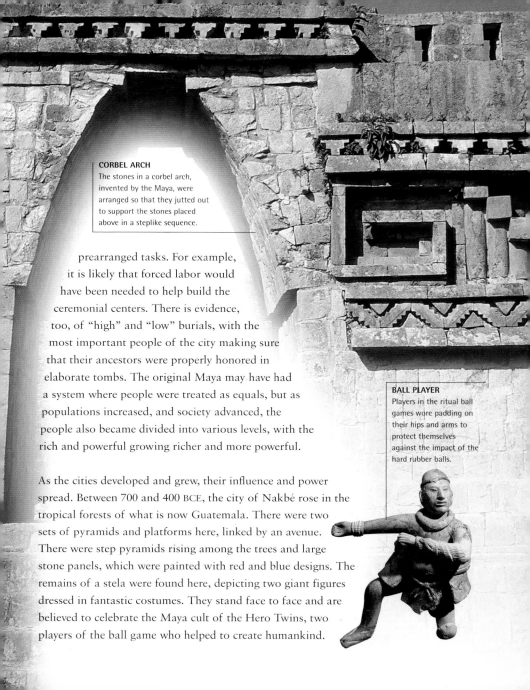

prearranged tasks. For example, it is likely that forced labor would have been needed to help build the ceremonial centers. There is evidence, too, of "high" and "low" burials, with the most important people of the city making sure that their ancestors were properly honored in elaborate tombs. The original Maya may have had a system where people were treated as equals, but as populations increased, and society advanced, the people also became divided into various levels, with the rich and powerful growing richer and more powerful.

As the cities developed and grew, their influence and power spread. Between 700 and 400 BCE, the city of Nakbé rose in the tropical forests of what is now Guatemala. There were two sets of pyramids and platforms here, linked by an avenue. There were step pyramids rising among the trees and large stone panels, which were painted with red and blue designs. The remains of a stela were found here, depicting two giant figures dressed in fantastic costumes. They stand face to face and are believed to celebrate the Maya cult of the Hero Twins, two players of the ball game who helped to create humankind.

WARLIKE MAYA
The ruler Chan Muan II
of Bonampak is shown
holding on to the hair
of a prisoner of war in
this famous Maya wall
painting. These scenes
reveal a warlike and
cruel side of the Maya.

Just north of Nakbé is the city of El Mirador, also now buried
within the jungle. It has been called Nakbé's "sister city" and is
linked to it by a giant causeway of limestone that cuts through the
trees and the undergrowth. There is a pyramid here, rising more than
60 ft (18 m) into the air. A wide staircase leads to a level area where
three temples were erected. On the base platform, from which the
staircase and the pyramid arise, are two other temples. They would
have been covered with lime plaster and painted red, yellow, and
blue. Images of the jaguar, with teeth and claws painted bright red,
have been found inside these structures. A short distance to the east
of this pyramid lies a compound of other pyramids and temples,
decorated with images of the vulture god and the jaguar god. Many
of these buildings remain unexplored. Perhaps there are others, still
unseen and unknown, in the vast cocoon of the jungle. El Mirador
was abandoned by its inhabitants approximately 800 years after its
foundation. Before they left it forever, the people engaged in the
ritual destruction of its temples and monuments.

It was once thought that the Maya, compared to the Aztecs, were a
peaceful and peace-loving people. But that illusion has now been
thoroughly dispelled. The Maya region may in fact have been
one of continual warfare. Stone monuments have been
found with stories of conflict and slaughter carved
upon them. The city of Becán, in the
lowlands, was fortified by a moat and
rampart (an earth mound) as well as a
timber fence, all of which suggests that the
Maya were ready to defend themselves against
enemies. The Maya may not have practiced human
sacrifice to the same extent as the Aztecs, but it was
still a part of their ritual calendar. They killed
women and children as part of their

ceremonies. The remains of 15 jaguars, which were sacrificed and then buried in a small tomb, have been found at one site. The Maya also engaged in ritual bloodletting to appease their gods. In that sense, they resembled the other cultures of Mesoamerica. There is even a Maya image showing the corpse of one human sacrifice being "bounced" down the steps of the pyramid in what might be considered typical Aztec fashion. The Maya tortured their victims before killing them, but they seem to have preferred beheading to the heart-tearing favored by the Aztecs.

BONAMPAK MURALS
This watercolor reconstruction shows noblemen wearing distinctive white cloaks and splendid headdresses during a Maya religious ceremony. It is based on an enormous mural discovered at Bonampak, near Yaxchilan, in 1946.

In a city called Bonampak were found some unique murals, dating from about 800 CE, that came as a revelation. There were images of music and dancing—the dancers wore monstrous masks, and the musicians used rattles and drums. But there were also more macabre images. There were scenes of torture and decapitation. There were prisoners with bleeding hands, their fingernails having been torn out. There were trials of captives. There was a king in full regalia, wearing a grotesque headdress of feathers as large as his own body. There was a boa constrictor in the headdress, too, to emphasize the leader's ferocity. These are not the images of a peace-loving race. They are images of power and conquest, of a people who were not only skilled architects, adventurous traders, and gifted artists, but who were ready and willing to impose their military might on those around them.

BONAMPAK MURALS
A line of colorfully clothed musicians and dancers forms a procession to celebrate the victory of one of their chiefs.

CHAPTER EIGHT

Maya scripts
and the stars

*When we think of what the Maya accomplished,
it is not necessarily their military might that first
comes to mind. Perhaps their most impressive
achievement was the development of a distinctive
and revolutionary form of hieroglyphic writing.*

ALTHOUGH THE OLMECS were probably the first
Mesoamericans to introduce a style of writing, it was
the Maya—some time between 50 BCE and 250 CE—
who developed it to a level not seen before in that part of the
world. The Maya writing system was made up of a selection
of more than 800 glyphs, or signs. Some glyphs represented
whole words or ideas, others just
individual syllables, rather like
today's Chinese script or the
hieroglyphs of the ancient Egyptians.
These Maya glyphs could be
endlessly combined or recombined to
form more complete or complex symbols, depending on what
the writer needed to say. It was an extremely difficult system
of representing language in which word and concept, picture
and sound were all mingled. It is, in fact, one of the
hallmarks of an advanced civilization and allows the Maya
to be grouped among the great cultures of the world.

◀ Detail from a Maya book, the *Codex Mendoza*

MAYA GLYPHS
Most glyphs are written in a square or rectangular shape, known as a cartouche.

The Maya often carved or sculpted these glyphs on the stone stelae that have been found in great numbers throughout the region. These glyphs recorded the dates and careers of individual leaders, together with information about alliances, wars, marriages, and who was next in line to become the king. From some, experts have been able to decipher the names of rulers such as Bird Jaguar, Smoking Squirrel, and Stormy Sky. The largest of these stone stelae, which rises some 35 ft (10.7 m) from the forest floor, shows the ruler, Cauac Sky, dressed in splendid ceremonial clothes.

MAYA BOOKS
Just four Maya books, or codices, still exist; this one is the *Codex Tro-Cortesianus.* It was read from top to bottom and left to right. The subject was divination (predicting the future) and rituals for Maya priests.

There are also books that display the writings of the Maya. These books were made from a single sheet of paper, sometimes many yards long, which was folded like an accordion to form separate pages. The paper itself was made from the pounded fiber of a fig tree that was coated with lime plaster to provide a smooth surface. Scribes then applied the glyphs in red or black paint using a fine-hair brush. The books were then given covers of wood or of jaguar skin.

The Spanish invaders burned hundreds, maybe thousands, of Maya books because they believed them to be the work of devils or magicians.

There were apparently works of history and genealogy, the calendar and numerology, but they have disappeared. That is why the Maya have remained such a mystery in the history of Mesoamerica. One collection of Maya myths and legends was acquired by a Dominican friar and copied out in Spanish. This is known as the *Popol Vuh* and describes the creation legends of the Maya. Although the original Maya manuscript has disappeared, this unique Spanish document is a reminder of all that has been lost.

WOMAN READING
Only a small number of people in Mesoamerica were taught to read. This woman must have been from the nobility to be shown holding a book.

KING OF TIKAL
Stormy Sky was one of Tikal's most successful rulers and built the city up to be one of the most powerful in the region. His elaborate headdress gave him extra prestige in the eyes of his people.

Only four Maya texts have survived. All four deal with aspects of ritual and astronomy. From studying these texts, historians have come to the conclusion that the Maya did not separate science and religion. Both were part of the Maya's overwhelming need to observe and to understand the workings of time. They possessed a calendar which, like that of the Aztecs, was made up of two different systems of counting the days of the year. One system comprised a solar year with 365 days divided into 18 months of 20 days, leaving five extra days that were considered unlucky. The other system was for religious purposes, with a year made up of 260 days. Only priests were trained to interpret this system, and people would consult them before important events.

WATCHING VENUS
The Maya were enthusiastic astronomers who were fascinated by the cycles of Venus. This page, from one of their books, shows a man observing that planet.

BRIGHT VENUS
Venus is the easiest planet to see from Earth. It is the brightest object in the night sky after the Moon.

It is reasonable to suggest that the Maya were obsessed with time—they worshiped it. They saw the days and years as living gods to be appeased and revered. The god of each date carried the burden of that date in a never-ending procession. Like other Mesoamerican cultures, the Maya saw the world proceeding in Great Cycles lasting for thousands of years, each ending with extinction and rebirth. Most scholars calculate that the present Great Cycle began on August 13, 3114 BCE. The Maya invented a system of notation called the Long Count as a way of showing the number of days that had passed since the beginning of the present Great Cycle. This cycle is due to end on December 21, 2012.

Another great achievement of Maya civilization lies in its feats of astronomical observation. Early astronomers must have watched the sky over many centuries, passing down their knowledge of the heavens from generation to generation. There are certain buildings in the ceremonial centers that would have been used as observatories, and there is evidence that the Maya used a kind of wooden device to take measurements of the Sun. They may even have used a form of magnetic compass. As a result of these measurements and observations, the Maya were able to chart accurately the movements of the planet Venus. They also measured the lunar month very precisely, and managed to successfully predict the time of a solar eclipse in their region of Earth, even though they were unaware, of course, that Earth revolved around the Sun.

The Maya view of the universe was a deeply religious one. To their mind, nature and the heavens were united, and the world was filled with gods. Their buildings were designed to repeat the pattern of the cosmos. You could say that their ceremonial centers were stone models of their beliefs. The central squares represented the surface of the underworld itself, and their pyramids copied the shapes of the sacred mountains that linked the earth with the sky. They performed elaborate ceremonies designed to reenact the process of creation.

The role of the priest, who performed many of these ceremonies, seems to have been inherited through families. Priests were trained in the various cultural practices of the Maya—to read and write, and to understand the movements of the sun, the moon, the planets, and the stars. They were also taught to prepare calendars, understand which dates were important, and, with the guidance

SOLAR ECLIPSE
The Maya knew enough about astronomy to predict an eclipse of the Sun. This happens when the Moon is in direct alignment with the Sun and Earth.

The Long Count

Maya priests believed that history was measured in Great Cycles, each 5,200 years long. To record time within these cycles, they used a system called the Long Count. This represented the number of days that had passed since the beginning of the current Great Cycle. Just as we have years, decades, and centuries, the Maya had five categories for measuring time:

1. Bak'tun (roughly 400 years)
2. K'atun (roughly 20 years)
3. Tun (360 days—roughly one year)
4. Winal (20 days—equivalent to a Maya month)
5. K'in (one day)

Many Maya stelae showed glyphs that represented the Long Count date. For example, this carving from Yaxchilan records that on 9.14.12.6.12 (February 12, 724 CE), Lord Shield Jaguar received a helmet from his wife, Lady Xoc. The complete date is shown in the T-shaped carving between the heads of the figures.

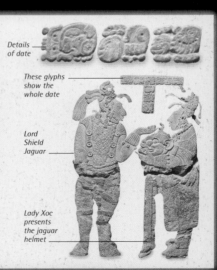

Details of date

These glyphs show the whole date

Lord Shield Jaguar

Lady Xoc presents the jaguar helmet

of the king, organize elaborate rituals. They performed their rites in temples that consisted of small narrow rooms, where darkness and secrecy were the essential elements. Caves and the wells known as cenotes, as we have seen, were also sacred places, linking the known and the unknown worlds. Offerings, such as small objects made of gold or copper (and sometimes humans), were thrown into the deep natural wells in order to please the gods. And there were many gods. One god might have different names and different appearances. There was the god of knowledge, and the god of death. There was a corn god. The sun and the moon were gods, and divine forces known as Chacs brought the rains and the thunder. The blood of each living thing was considered to be holy.

Out of this array of gods the Maya fashioned a system of belief, and a system of correct behavior or ethics. They apologized to the gods of the soil before clearing the ground, and to the god of corn before reaping the harvest. In their personal conduct, they were taught to be moderate and tolerant in their dealings. They were instructed to remain calm, to conceal their feelings, and to work harmoniously with each other. Their capacity to work hard together must have been one of the reasons for the great flowering of Maya civilization in what has become known as the Classic period, approximately 250–1000 CE. In one sense, this period is simply an intensification of what had come before—more temples, more palaces, and more stelae. But this was also the time when dynasties or ruling families appeared. It was the age of kingship, of the holy lords known as *k'ul ahaws*.

DEATH MASK
Powerful leaders had special funerals. The Maya buried their kings wearing jade death masks, like this one. The Maya believed that after death, they continued with their earthly role. A king was still a king, a slave still a slave.

A great example of Maya abilities can be found in the rise of the city-state known as Tikal. This was one of the first Maya settlements to develop into a city. It was first started as a farming community, but by the 2nd century BCE, workers had constructed a large pyramid and a central ritual area. This remained a ceremonial site for the next 900 years, with burial tombs and temples being constructed and reconstructed on the same ground.

Tikal reached its first peak between 250 and 600 CE. It was not arranged in the grid pattern that Aztec cities adopted, but was more spread out. It can best be described as a series of concentric rings, with the city at the center controlling or administering a large region around it. The leaders and the elite lived closest to the center. The ritual area was, after all, the source of power. But there were suburbs, some intensely populated, as well as farms and villages in a dependent relationship with the center. In this, Tikal is typical of Maya cities, which seem in many instances to take on the role of regional capitals. Tikal also seems to have controlled other cities in its region of influence. There were some cities whose zones of influence covered many different kinds of territory, ranging from limestone hills to tropical rainforests and swamps. The whole region would have been linked with ties of trade as well as of administration.

Tikal itself covered an area of 6 square miles (16 sq km). It has been estimated that there were something like 3,000 structures within the city at this time, supporting a population of some 10,000 people. There were areas for officials and for priests, with evidence of high-status houses. There were smaller houses for less important citizens.

FAMILY HOMES
Maya homes had no doors or private spaces, but strings of bells across the doorways warned when someone was entering. This lack of privacy was not a problem because the Maya were used to communal living. This modern Maya home is like those of the early Maya.

There were quarters devoted to craft-workers, such as those working in obsidian or jade. At the heart of the city were the public buildings devoted to power and worship. These are now covered by the canopy of the tropical forests, mute reminders of their glory, but it is possible in imagination to see them once again resplendent in a gleaming white city.

There are many temples, the tallest of which rose some 200 ft (60 m), and there are many palaces or administrative buildings grouped around courtyards. There are special courts for the playing of the ritual ball game. There are stairways and platforms and great doorways, all originally covered in a fine white plaster and decorated with murals of the gods. All these buildings were erected on high ground, above the swampy condition of the territory, and were linked by causeways of limestone. It was an immense architectural and social achievement, in the face of natural conditions that would normally restrict the progress of civilized life. One area of Tikal is known as Mundo Perdido or "lost world." Archaeologists gave it this name as a reminder of the many stories that have been told about lost, or unknown, peoples—which is what the Maya themselves once were.

RAINFOREST AND SWAMP
Tikal was a combination of city and swamp. Situated in the heart of Guatemala's tropical rainforest, stone structures and stelae were built between sections of uninhabitable marshland.

MAYA WOMEN
Archaeologists have found decorated vases at various Maya sites. These help them to understand more about how the Maya looked, as well as how they lived. The woman on this vase, for example, wears an elaborate headdress as well as earrings, possibly made of shell.

THE REMAINS OF TIKAL
Many of the ruins of Tikal remain hidden by jungle
undergrowth. The central square, and some of its
impressive pyramids, however, can still be
recognized. Stone stelae that recorded the lives of
the city's rulers can be seen in the foreground.

CHAPTER NINE

Of kings *and*
conquests

Maya kings were dynamic rulers who held the keys to power and conquest. They enriched their cities, extended their kingdoms, and battled each other for survival. But Maya society gradually grew weak, until this great civilization mysteriously disappeared.

THE SOCIAL STRUCTURE OF the Maya was like one of the pyramids in their great cities. At the top was the king, who was responsible for pleasing the gods and defending the realm. Beneath him were the nobles and the priestly elite who might have also been scribes or astrologers. Next came the palace officials, who organized and controlled the administration of the kingdom. Then there were merchants and craftsmen, among whom were woodcarvers and tailors, weavers and stonemasons. Beneath them in the social hierarchy came the farmers. And beneath them came the serfs or laborers and, finally, the slaves. While the king lived in a grand palace, the ordinary Maya lived in single-room dwellings. These were built with walls of mud brick and roofs of thatch made from palm leaves.

◄ A decorated pyramid from Palenque

CITY IN THE FOREST
This scene shows how the powerful city of Palenque might have looked, set among the tropical vegetation. The great Maya ruler Pakal was responsible for most of the pyramids and palaces that made the city so distinctive.

An extended farming family, for example, might have several such dwellings arranged around a simple courtyard. Archaeologists found one Maya house of the 5th century CE in a good state of preservation, buried under a layer of volcanic ash. The site revealed pots of beans as well as corn plants still standing in the field. The Maya were very good farmers, and even in the less-than-ideal conditions of the rainforest, they managed to provide enough surplus food for the populations of the great cities. Their diet included all the local plants and vegetables—corn, beans, squash, chili peppers—but on occasions they also ate monkeys and birds, deer and large rodents called agouti, which they caught and killed using dogs, clubs, traps, and snares. Like other people in Mesoamerica, the Maya ate a breed of hairless dog, which was raised specifically as food. And they loved turkey stew.

Maya people wore simple clothing made of woven fabric or animal
skins. The men wore a loincloth and the women a type of tunic with an
underskirt. Both wrapped cloaks around themselves in colder weather.
The clothes of the nobility were, of course, more elaborate and would
have been richly colored using natural plant and animal dyes. The Maya
also wore bracelets, necklaces, and earrings and had holes pierced in
their noses, ears, and lips for the insertion of ornaments. Tattooing and
body painting were also practiced.

The art of the Maya has not survived well in the heat and humidity of
the rainforest. Some vivid wall paintings still exist, as we have seen from
the city of Bonampak, and they reveal a great deal about the style used
by the Maya artists. Their art is full of detail, and artists put meaning

HUNTING FOR FOOD
This plate shows a Maya
hunting scene. The man in
the center carries a deer he
has caught. Hunters often
used dogs to help them
catch deer and wild pigs.

into every image. This explains why the headdress of a ruler or a deity is generally shown to be enormous, because it marks the status and the role of the figure. The position in which a figure stood and the way in which the arms were held all meant something, too. Noble figures appear larger than others, while a bird might be the same size as a tree. Many Maya paintings and sculptures were placed in temples and were only ever intended to be seen by the gods.

SKIRTS AND SHAWLS
This Maya woman wears a matching patterned skirt and shawl. Her hair ribbons, bracelet, and feather earrings are typical of the fashion for personal decoration.

BIRDS ON A POT
Maya potters, mostly women, worked with coils of wet clay or with molds. The birds that decorate this cooking pot are images of the quetzal bird.

Craftsman or king, priest or farmer—as a Maya, your role in life would have been determined by your birth. Being able to trace your descent from both your mother and father was very important and determined your position in society and whom you would be allowed to marry. If your parents were members of powerful and important families, it is likely you would be powerful and important, too, and would be given a high position. Kings also usually inherited their role, but this was not always the case. In the city of Tikal, there is a break in the succession of kings after the reign of Great Jaguar Paw. Instead of being succeeded by his son, Great Jaguar Paw was followed by Curl Nose, a ruler who seems to have come from far-

LIVING BY THE RIVER
Only Maya kings and priests lived in the city centers. Most of the people lived in the surrounding countryside. This wall painting from Chichén Itzá shows the typical thatched homes on the banks of a river teeming with fish.

distant Teotihuacan. This period in Tikal's history is sometimes called the Teotihuacan takeover. As we have seen, Teotihuacan was the capital of all capitals in Mesoamerica, and it is no wonder that its influence spread to the Maya. New styles of pottery and of architecture created at Teotihuacan are also found in Tikal. This was partly a result of the trade routes established between the different cultures of Mesoamerica, and, of course, between the different cities of the Maya. There were trade routes for pottery and for slaves, for cotton and for honey, for salt and for metal. But the fact that Tikal was so significantly influenced by Teotihuacan suggests some closer alliance—perhaps through a successful invasion or as a result of marriage between the families of the rulers of both cities. There is no actual evidence to support this, but just as the Olmecs affected the development of cultures in regions other than their own, so the influence of Teotihuacan spread far beyond its boundaries.

But there were conflicts as well as alliances. City would fight against city for superiority. There was a period when Tikal was highly successful. It seemed to have gained authority over many neighboring cities or kingdoms. But it also had formidable and powerful enemies. Among the most important of these was the city of Calakmul, which lay some 60 miles (100 km) north of Tikal. Calakmul was even larger than Tikal, with its own palaces, pyramids, and temples. There were 6,000 separate structures in the central area of the city, which suggests a very large population.

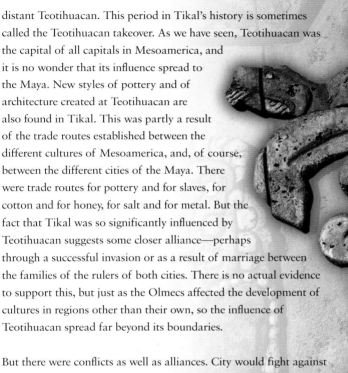

KING BIRD JAGUAR
Maya kings commissioned great statues of themselves so they would be remembered after death. Bird Jaguar of Yaxchilán shows off all his finest jewelry.

Stone rings were positioned more than 20 ft (6 m) above the court.

Special ball courts were built in the ceremonial centers of each city.

Ritual ball game

The ball game was not a simple sport but a religious event that was played throughout Mesoamerica. It was a rough and tough game that could end in death for the losers. The game involved two players, or teams of players, who competed to see who could propel a hard rubber ball through one of the stone rings set on either side of the court. Players were only allowed to use their hips, knees, and elbows to move the ball.

This image shows blood spurting from the neck of a player who lost a game.

Ball players, usually noblemen, wore specially padded clothing to protect themselves from the fast-moving ball. The games were hugely popular, and people came to watch and to place bets on who would win or die.

ENTRANCE TO THE UNDERWORLD
A sculpture of the storm god was found at the Temple of the Inscriptions in Copán. He stands on a ball court and is thought to symbolize the entrance to the underworld.

Recent archaeological investigation seems to prove that there was an ongoing war between Tikal and Calakmul. And then, in 562 CE, Tikal was overthrown by Calakmul. There was widespread looting and demolition within the capital. Monuments were defaced and the sculptures knocked down. As a result of this victory, Calakmul came to dominate the entire area through a mixture of power politics and dynastic marriages. But Tikal was not entirely defeated. Although its leaders were probably executed or sacrificed, the city itself continued to be inhabited. It had been humiliated, but, as we will see, one day it rose again.

At the time of Tikal's defeat, there is a gap of some 60 years in the historical record. This period is marked by the absence both of stelae and of ceremonial building in the lowlands of the Maya region. We know of no real explanation for this gap— at least not yet. After this pause, however, comes the peak of Maya culture, which lasted from approximately 600 to 1000 CE.

In this era, the cities of the Maya became richer, more complex, and more powerful. Old cities were renewed, and new cities flourished. Not all of the Maya people would have lived in great cities such as Tikal. It has been estimated that the total population of the Maya, in the 8th century, was some 10 million. It was one of the largest civilizations in the world. Evidence of more than 40 cities has been found, each with its own regional style, religious beliefs, and ceremonial practices. But despite these differences, there also seems to have been some competition between rival cities to build the most elaborate temples and the highest pyramids. We may take as examples the city of Copán in the east, and the city of Palenque in the west.

Copán was not the largest city, but it was the most spectacular and impressive of all the Maya centers. A very large ball court has been found, decorated with great stone heads of the macaw bird. There is a remarkable statue of the storm god, holding a torch. There are carvings of strange beasts from Maya myth and legend. There is a temple built in the shape of a mountain with a huge monster mouth as its entrance. There is a grand Hieroglyphic Stairway with more than 2,000 inscriptions carved upon its steps, which retell the history of the Copán kingdom. And there are some of the largest and most magnificent stelae in the Maya world. From their inscriptions we can learn something of the Copán dynasty,

FACE OF STONE
This stone carving reveals the face of King 18 Rabbit of Copán. He is shown here as the god of corn, who was thought to have danced during the creation of the world.

HIEROGLYPHIC STAIRWAY
This stone stairway is inscribed with hieroglyphs that mark out Copán's history. Portraits of rulers can be found at intervals of every 12 steps.

REMAINS OF PALENQUE
The ruins of this ancient city were first discovered in 1773. Many of the monuments that can be seen today, such as the palace and Temple of the Inscriptions (shown here), date from the reign of the ruler Pakal.

which included such kings as Moon Jaguar, Smoke Jaguar, 18 Rabbit, Smoke Monkey, and Smoke Shell. Each king in turn decorated and renovated and extended his city kingdom. Temples were built upon older temples, and burial chambers covered in frescoes were laid out for the esteemed dead. As Copán prospered, so did the city of Palenque. It is situated in the foothills of the Chiapas Mountains, overlooking the coastal plain stretching down to the Gulf of Mexico. It rose to prominence as a regional center around the 7th century. The scale of its achievement was not really understood until it was discovered in recent years, and even today parts of the city are still obscured by jungle

foliage. Palaces with painted walls have been found here, with council chambers, burial chambers, temples with great limestone panels carved with inscriptions and images, and stairways carved with glyphs. There are painted images of the royal succession, which are illuminated once a year by the dying sun of the winter solstice. At this time, a beam of sunlight follows the line of pyramid steps down to the burial chamber of the most revered ruler of Palenque, Pakal. The king is the sun itself, its rays tracing his steps down to the underworld. The burial chamber of Pakal was discovered in 1949, but it took three years of patient excavation for its secrets to be revealed. A trap door of limestone was found in the inner sanctum of a temple pyramid. Beneath this trap door was a staircase leading down to a small chamber where five or six people had been ritually murdered. There was a triangular slab in the wall behind them that was, in essence, a stone doorway. Behind the stone slab was a sarcophagus, containing the skeleton of the great king covered with jewelry and ornaments of jade. The lid of the sarcophagus had been inscribed with an image of Pakal lying on top of the setting sun as it travels down into the waiting jaws of the underworld. There was enough here to challenge the greatest of the Egyptian burials in the Valley of the Kings, and it proved beyond doubt that the Maya civilization was, at its height, one of awesome power and wealth.

The inscriptions show that Palenque was in close alliance with the city of Tikal, which, after its apparent demise in the middle of the 6th century, once again rose to prominence as part of the general revival of the Maya city-states in the 7th century. Under the rule of the king known as Shield Skull and his descendants, Tikal extended its power through the southern lowlands and its range of influence over a wider area still. Tikal fought against Calakmul and defeated it in battle—the Calakmul leaders were taken for sacrifice in Tikal. The rulers engaged in a massive program of reconstruction and rebuilding. The Great Plaza and the North Acropolis were rebuilt after the previous desecrations. Six new large temples were constructed, as well as the complex known as Twin Pyramids. The limestone causeways were extended, and existing structures were enlarged and enriched. The tallest building of the Maya world, and some of the highest structures in all of Mesoamerica, are to be found in Tikal. But then the trail falls silent. Its historical record becomes a blank. It disappears from the stage of the world.

DEATH OF PAKAL
When the ruler Pakal died, his ornamented body was placed in a sarcophagus (top). This was protected by a stone slab decorated with the figure of Pakal and various star signs. The jade funeral mask (above) was placed over the dead king's face.

The great city of Palenque seems to have been one of the first of the Maya cities to vanish from history in the 9th century. There were no more buildings, and no more monuments. The leaders seem to have been swept away, and the ceremonial centers left in ruins. The populations declined, died, or moved on. The list of abandoned cities is a long one—Bonampak, Palenque, Copán, Calakmul, Tikal, and scores of others. By the beginning of the 10th century, there was not one surviving major center. The ruins of these cities were not seen again until almost 1,000 years later, when they excited wonder from the 20th-century archaeologists who rediscovered them. The collapse extended beyond the southern lowlands. By the 10th century, highland settlements had also been abandoned, and the population sought refuge in more defensible locations. Some of the northern cities also declined.

Many reasons have been given for this general Maya collapse. Some think it was the result of epidemic disease, or of an earthquake. Others point to the possible invasion of foreign peoples. It has been suggested that the laboring peasant populations of these mighty cities rose up in revolt against their masters, who were building their great temples and palaces on the backs and the sweat of the poor. Others have suggested periods of widespread drought, crop failures, and subsequent food shortages. And so occurred one of the most extraordinary collapses in human history.

CHICHÉN ITZÁ
This city shows the mingling of Maya and Toltec styles. The pyramid of El Castillo (below right) was dedicated to the cult of Kukulkan, the Maya equivalent of the Toltec Feathered Serpent, Quetzalcoatl. In the foreground, the figure of a chacmool holds a bowl for offerings to the gods.

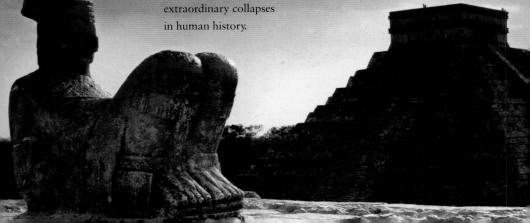

In the period that followed, the Yucatán was the only region that flourished. Peoples known as the Putun and the Itzá came to dominate the trade of the region. There is one city, Chichén Itzá, that is remarkable because it combines both Toltec and Maya styles. After the demise of Chichén Itzá, the city of Mayapan became the dominant power in northern Yucatán. But it was not as well-structured as earlier cities—the architecture was not of the same quality and it had no ball court. The game had fallen out of favor. Its absence may also be an indication that the religious framework of Maya society was not as strong as it had once been.

Like so many other cities of Mesoamerica, Mayapan had a fiery and destructive end. In approximately 1450 CE, the ceremonial center was looted and the dwellings burned. It is true that the pattern of most Maya city-states had been one of rise and fall and rise again, but this time there was to be no more resurrection. After the demise of Mayapan, the area dissolved into communities that were isolated and relatively defenseless by the time the Spaniards invaded. The Spaniards, however, did not conquer the entire region for many years. They were hindered by the variable terrain, and they never ventured far into the rainforests. And yet, after centuries of colonization and victimization, the Maya survived. The descendants of the people who built Palenque and Copán still live in Guatemala and eastern Mexico, Honduras and Belize. They eat much the same food and share many of the same customs as their distant ancestors. They worship in some of the same sacred places. In parts of Guatemala, they even use the old calendar of 260 days. It represents an astonishing continuity of more than 4,000 years, in the face of overwhelming odds of decline and conquest. In celebrating the Maya, we are celebrating the persistence of life itself.

END OF AN ERA
Scientists believe that severe droughts may have contributed to the decline of the Maya. Without crops for food and water for drinking, people would not have survived. Other possible reasons include earthquakes or the spread of disease.

CHAPTER TEN

Lords *of the* Andes

Dominated by the great Andes Mountains, the vast empire of the Inca was linked by an intricate system of twisting roads and rope bridges. The rulers, too, believed they were linked to the sun god Inti, which gave them absolute power over their people.

THERE WAS ONLY ONE OTHER early American civilization that could rival those of the Olmecs, the Aztecs, and the Maya. It lay farther south than these kingdoms, down the western side of the South American continent. It was the land and empire of the people we know as the Inca. When the Spaniards invaded this land in 1531, the Inca Empire was the largest in the southern hemisphere. It covered modern-day Peru, Bolivia, Ecuador, and stretched almost to the south of Colombia, the north of Chile, and into parts of Argentina. It encompassed mountains and deserts, sea coasts and tropical jungles. It included the green rainforests of the Amazon and the great white peaks of the Andes Mountains. The empire was known as *Tahuantinsuyu*, which means "the Land of the Four Quarters" in the native Quechua language.

◀ Inca steps carved into the steep slopes of the Andes

The empire was divided into four regions by four great highways that radiated out from the center of the capital city, Cuzco—the very heart of the Inca world. The word "Inca" means "supreme ruler" and was the name used by the native Quechua people for their king. The Spaniards later applied the name to all the people of the Inca's empire. This territory stretched some 3,000 miles (4,800 k) from north to south, and was inhabited by approximately 8–10 million people. How was it that this vast empire and huge population was conquered and then governed by a relatively small number of Inca people? It is one of the most interesting stories in all of human history.

CHIMU GOLDSMITHS
This gold ear ornament, with a warrior holding a victim's head, was made by Chimu goldsmiths. Their empire was conquered by the Inca.

The Inca were, originally, one of many peoples who inhabited the region around the Andes Mountains. In approximately 1000 CE, they fought their way down into the fertile valley of Cuzco, and from here they began the territorial expansion that would, within 500 years, create their giant empire.
The Inca were not, of course, the first successful or civilized inhabitants of this region of South America. Before them, there were the Nazca, the Moche, and the Chimu, who lived along the Pacific coast. Farther inland were the Chavín and the Tiahuanaco. The Inca were, in fact, the last great example of a succession of cultures that had existed, in various forms, for many thousands of years in this region of South America.

MOCHE PORTRAIT
This pre-Inca pottery vessel, made by the Moche culture, shows the almond-shaped eyes and brown skin typical of the Andean people.

The earliest Inca settlers were engaged in endless warfare with neighboring peoples known as the Chanca and Ayarmaca. They eventually defeated these peoples and began the process of colonization and expansion that was to result in the Inca Empire. Before beginning a course of conquest of other areas, however, they took firm control over their local territory. As part of this same curve of ambition, they began to construct their elaborate capital city—Cuzco, the Navel of the Universe—and to decorate it with the architecture of power, such as temples and palaces. This period of empire building probably lasted some 200 years from 1200 to 1400 CE. During this time, many local warring tribes were defeated and their leaders sacrificed. Much booty was taken in the process, and this new-found wealth was used to help create the great capital at Cuzco.

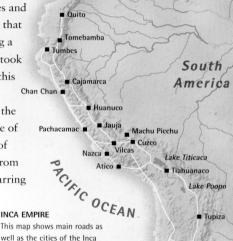

CARIBBEAN SEA

South America

PACIFIC OCEAN

Quito
Tomebamba
Tumbes
Cajamarca
Chan Chan
Huanuco
Pachacamac
Jauja
Machu Picchu
Cuzco
Nazca
Vilcas
Atico
Lake Titicaca
Tiahuanaco
Lake Poopo
Tupiza
Pucara de Andalgala
Talca

INCA EMPIRE
This map shows main roads as well as the cities of the Inca and their predecessors.

Nazca lines

Giant hands
This outline of two hands is one of many Nazca geoglyphs. They were first noticed when planes flew over in the 1920s.

The people known as the Nazca drew vast drawings on the rocky surface of the desert between the coast of Peru and the Andes. They are called earth-drawings, or geoglyphs, and they cover a huge area. They were created between 200 BCE and 600 CE, although they may have been retraced from an earlier era. They form many different shapes, including a monkey, a hummingbird, a spider, and a whale. The surprising feature of these "lines" is that they can only be identified from the air. No one is certain how they were made.

Hummingbird

Monkey

There were three emperors of the new empire:
Pachacuti, Topa Inca, and Huayna Capac, although
we also know the names and exploits of eight earlier rulers
of Cuzco (some possibly mythical, others clearly historical
figures). These included Viracocha, who named himself after
the Inca creator god, and ruled before the empire was established.
By consolidating Inca power in the Cuzco region, Viracocha helped
to pave the way for his successors. The first of these, Pachacuti,
embarked upon a campaign of foreign conquest that initiated the
Inca Empire. He then handed all military power to his son, Topa
Inca. Meanwhile, Pachacuti concentrated on a great reordering of
the Inca state. He laid out the capital city, Cuzco, and introduced a
program of road-building and a form of taxation. Pachacuti was one
of those compelling national leaders, like Simón Bolívar or George
Washington, who carve out a nation's destiny.

His son and successor, Topa Inca, was a stunningly successful
military commander who extended the empire from Ecuador to
northern Chile. He waged many wars and invaded many different
lands. In the process he conquered the other great state of South
America—Chimor, the capital of which was Chan Chan.

Topa Inca's successor, Huayna Capac, strengthened the empire from within and maintained its existing power. He was a ferocious and determined leader. After one victory over a group of rebellious subjects, he decapitated all the rebels and threw them into a lake—it has been known as "the lake of blood" ever since. In more peaceful times he resolved disputes between neighboring lords. Huayna Capac also conducted grand tours of his kingdom in order to improve the way the empire was run. He was the last Inca to rule an undivided kingdom. After his death, a civil war broke out between his two sons, an unhappy situation that was exploited by the invading Spaniards.

During the reigns of Topa Inca and Huayna Capac, the organization of the empire was firmly established. The Inca emperors appointed the lords of each conquered city or locality, and sometimes forced them to live in Cuzco as a guarantee of their loyalty. In the course of a mere 100 years, the emperors established an empire of astonishing size and diversity. It was to the emperors' advantage that their subjects were divided among themselves. They lived in many city-states, and seem to have been engaged in intermittent or perpetual rivalry with one another. By force or bribery, by threat or other means of persuasion, the emperors forged these little states into administrative and territorial units under their control. The local leaders and their people were allowed to keep their own customs and gods as long as they pledged allegiance to the Inca lord

EMPEROR'S CLOTHES
This Inca poncho-and-headdress set was made from the feathers of tropical birds, and would have been worn by an emperor. The pattern shows images of owls and fish.

and fulfilled the obligations imposed upon them. But in order to unify the various lands and tribes that they conquered, the Inca imposed one language upon all. It was their own language, now known as Quechua, and it is still spoken today.

OLD INCA TRAILS
The trail to the Inca fortress of Machu Picchu remains a challenge today. The narrow path and vertical cliff edges are breathtaking.

This empire could not, however, have been held together by language alone. The true genius of the Inca lay in their solution to the real problems of empire-building. Of course, they did not come up with these ideas on their own, but developed and extended the ideas of the people who had come before them. The Inca were, like some of their predecessors, aware of the need for swift communication between the distant parts of the empire. So they built a sophisticated system of roads that can still be traced today through jungles and over mountain ranges. A 19th-century explorer was one of the first Europeans to come upon an old Inca road, about 10 ft (3 m) wide, paved and bordered with stones, which descended some 4,000 ft (1,220 m) into a deep valley. Other roads that have since been discovered were lined with walls and shaded by trees. In the flat desert areas, the route was marked by piles of stones. Two main highways ran from north to south—one through the mountainous region and one through the low coastal plains—and were

linked to each other by numerous smaller roads. The roads ran for vast distances throughout the territory of the Inca—estimated at some 20,000 miles (32,000 km) in total—and were used for the distribution of goods as well as to keep channels of communication open between different parts of the empire. There were even roads reserved for certain types of trade or occupation, and a traveler on the wrong road could be sentenced to death.

Where gorges and ravines made roads impossible, the Inca built bridges of logs or braided plant fiber. There were rope bridges spanning deep canyons, sometimes covering distances of 200–300 ft (60–90 m). Other bridges were made from cables stretched across a river or gorge, with baskets suspended from them. People or objects were placed in the

ROAD MAP
The Inca roads provided an essential link between highland and coastal populations and also for moving people to new homes within the empire.

ACROSS THE RIVER
Bridges made from braided plant fiber, like this one, were built to cross rivers and gorges. Laborers guarded the bridges to make safety checks and look for signs of wear.

ROAD RUNNERS
Inca runners who carried messages and supplies across the empire were called *chasquis*, from the word for "exchange." A relay team could cover 150 miles (240 km) in a day.

baskets, which were then pulled across the river or gorge from the other side. And this amazing network is how the state messengers, called *chasquis*, running in relays, could reach any part of the kingdom in a relatively short time. Fish caught off the Pacific coast, for example, could be transported across the mountains and still be fresh by the time it reached the inland city of Cuzco.

STONE STOREHOUSE
The Inca built solid stone storehouses where they kept a permanent supply of provisions for people, such as soldiers, traveling on the road network.

Along the roads there were taverns or, lodging houses, known as *tambos*, where travelers could rest. There were also great stone storehouses, known as *colla*, which were used to store food and provisions for those who used the road network. These storehouses not only supplied food for the emperor and his retinue but, perhaps more importantly, they provided sustenance for the great armies that followed the stone roads into the most distant parts of the empire. The storehouses were sturdy and well-ventilated buildings, and workers constructed many thousands of them, often on hillsides where they were easy to see. They were emblems of Inca power and efficiency. They also became emblems of power in another sense, since the local farmers were required to keep the storehouses well-supplied with goods for the empire. Foodstuffs and produce from all over the empire—dried meat,

The roads were also used to transport the large groups of people who were forced by the emperor to move to other areas. These Inca colonists, or *mitmacs*, were often forced to resettle in newly conquered lands. They took everything with them to their new homes, including their Inca customs and beliefs. This proved an effective way of spreading Inca ideas as well as the Quechua language. Correspondingly, the children of conquered rulers were sent to Cuzco to be educated, then returned to their native lands to become rulers loyal to the Inca. The Inca were remarkably clever at what we would now term social engineering.

As with the people, the land itself was also organized and controlled. Farmers were moved from high lands of pasture to lower farm lands so that every level could be used to grow various crops. Tubers or root vegetables were grown at higher altitudes, cacao and cotton at lower levels. In the mountain regions, the farmers created stepped terraces in the steep hillsides to grow corn and other important crops. These terraces are still used today by local farmers. Potatoes, a type of tuber, were also grown at high altitude, and provided one of the staples of the Inca diet. It was the Inca, in fact, who introduced the humble potato to the world.

STEEP TERRACES
Farmers cut terraces into the steep hillsides, which would otherwise be unusable. These fields were watered by a system of irrigation channels.

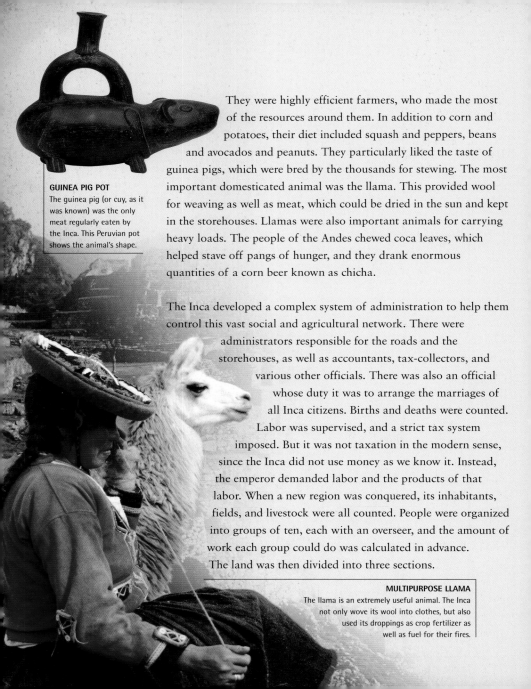

GUINEA PIG POT
The guinea pig (or cuy, as it was known) was the only meat regularly eaten by the Inca. This Peruvian pot shows the animal's shape.

They were highly efficient farmers, who made the most of the resources around them. In addition to corn and potatoes, their diet included squash and peppers, beans and avocados and peanuts. They particularly liked the taste of guinea pigs, which were bred by the thousands for stewing. The most important domesticated animal was the llama. This provided wool for weaving as well as meat, which could be dried in the sun and kept in the storehouses. Llamas were also important animals for carrying heavy loads. The people of the Andes chewed coca leaves, which helped stave off pangs of hunger, and they drank enormous quantities of a corn beer known as chicha.

The Inca developed a complex system of administration to help them control this vast social and agricultural network. There were administrators responsible for the roads and the storehouses, as well as accountants, tax-collectors, and various other officials. There was also an official whose duty it was to arrange the marriages of all Inca citizens. Births and deaths were counted. Labor was supervised, and a strict tax system imposed. But it was not taxation in the modern sense, since the Inca did not use money as we know it. Instead, the emperor demanded labor and the products of that labor. When a new region was conquered, its inhabitants, fields, and livestock were all counted. People were organized into groups of ten, each with an overseer, and the amount of work each group could do was calculated in advance. The land was then divided into three sections.

MULTIPURPOSE LLAMA
The llama is an extremely useful animal. The Inca not only wove its wool into clothes, but also used its droppings as crop fertilizer as well as fuel for their fires.

QUECHUA CHILDREN
When they were two years old, Inca children went to a ceremony in which a lock of their hair was cut. Their time as a baby came to an end.

One section was allocated to the gods, and the food produced on it was given to the priests or used on religious holidays. Another section belonged to the emperor himself, and the produce from this was used to fill the storehouses and support the people in government and royal court. The last section was communal land, where the people labored separately for their own needs. This agricultural labor was one type of tax. Another form of tax was known as *mit'a* service, in which all fit and able men had to devote a certain amount of time laboring on the great buildings and enterprises of the Inca Empire. The third system of taxation was one in which Inca women wove cloth that was placed in the great storehouses to be distributed or exchanged for other goods. The emperor, therefore, developed a grand program of redistribution, in which the various products of the realm were circulated by means of trade and by means of the storehouses.

As in earlier Andean civilizations, the Inca also used a system of exchange, known as "reciprocity," which worked at every level of society. At a local level, family groups, known as *ayllus*, helped each other with tasks that an individual family could not manage alone. At a higher level, the emperor and his representatives gave favors and presents in exchange for tribute. Presents were also lavished on local lords, who provided food and drink to the local people at times of celebration. This vast network of connections and exchanges also helped to ensure that the storehouses were always full. In this way, the Inca rulers were able to maintain and support a vast population.

WEAVING AND TEXTILES
Most weaving took place in the outer courtyards of homes. Women carried their weaving tools and cotton threads in reed baskets. When women died, these baskets were often buried with them so that they could weave in the afterlife.

CHAPTER ELEVEN

Cities *in the* sky

Religious ceremonies to worship the sun and rituals to honor the dead took place high in the sacred Inca cities. But this isolated existence was to last no more than 400 years. Invaders from Spain brought disease and death to the people and to the empire.

A S THEIR EMPIRE GREW EVER LARGER, the Inca built a number of great cities and fortresses in many of their dependent territories. These cities served as centers for both religious and government activities, and were well-stocked with storehouses full of provisions. But the Inca lavished most attention upon their own cities.

The capital, Cuzco, was deemed to be sacred. It was a walled city, built in a valley among the mountains. The layout was said to follow the shape of a puma, with the great fortress of Sacsahuaman forming its head. The walls of Sacsahuaman stand to this day. Inside Cuzco there were vast plazas and palaces, fountains and temples. From their elevated position, more than 11,000 ft (3,350 m) above sea level, these buildings often touched— or rose above—the clouds. At the heart of the city was the Haucaypata, or Holy Place. This was an open plaza where

◄ The fortress city of Machu Picchu, Peru

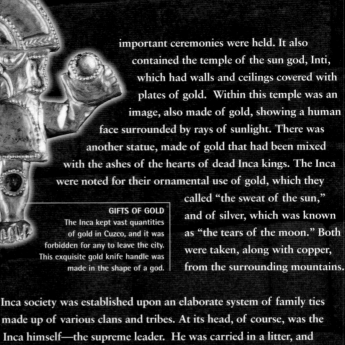

important ceremonies were held. It also contained the temple of the sun god, Inti, which had walls and ceilings covered with plates of gold. Within this temple was an image, also made of gold, showing a human face surrounded by rays of sunlight. There was another statue, made of gold that had been mixed with the ashes of the hearts of dead Inca kings. The Inca were noted for their ornamental use of gold, which they called "the sweat of the sun," and of silver, which was known as "the tears of the moon." Both were taken, along with copper, from the surrounding mountains.

GIFTS OF GOLD
The Inca kept vast quantities of gold in Cuzco, and it was forbidden for any to leave the city. This exquisite gold knife handle was made in the shape of a god.

Inca society was established upon an elaborate system of family ties made up of various clans and tribes. At its head, of course, was the Inca himself—the supreme leader. He was carried in a litter, and children were employed to sweep the ground before him. His earrings were great discs of gold. His bodyguards were clothed in sheets of gold. It was assumed that the Inca would marry his sister in order to maintain the power of the royal line. Although he had many wives, only a son of his sister-wife (who was known as Coya, or empress) could be the next emperor. The emperor was the child of the sun, and any lord approaching him was required to carry a burden on his back as a sign of humility.

BUILT TO LAST
The remains of the stone walls still stand at the fortress of Sacsahuaman. Inca architects cut huge stone slabs so that they fitted together perfectly.

Beneath the emperor in the social order were the immediate members of the royal family. Then there were the lords and noble families who helped to administer the empire. After these came the priests and the administrators, the technicians and the traders, while below them were the common folk, made up of peasant farmers and fishermen. No one in the centrally controlled Inca territories was allowed to own land—as we know, they were only given rights to use plots for the purpose of growing food. The servants of the Inca nobles were known as *yanas* and inherited their positions. It was considered a privilege to serve their masters.

The buildings of Cuzco confirm that the Inca were extraordinary engineers and architects. The fortress of Sacsahuaman is built from great blocks of shaped stone, some of them weighing about 300 tons. No cement or mortar was used in the construction, but the blocks were cut so accurately, using tools of stone or bronze, that they locked into one another. These massive blocks were placed in position so precisely that the blade of a knife cannot be inserted between them. That is why they are still standing. Even tremors from occasional earthquakes only caused the rocks to shudder and then settle back into place. Yet it is still not known how the Inca managed to lift and place these stones into their exact positions. They had no wheels to transport them.

GONE TO THE GRAVE
These dolls, dressed in typical clothes, were excavated from the world's highest archaeological site, in Peru. They were found alongside a sacrificed Inca child.

It is also presumed that the Inca did not use
writing. Instead, in common with a number of
other Andean peoples, they used an ingenious
system of recording information by means of knotted
strings. This system is known as a *quipu* and can be
described as the language of knots. This way of keeping
records could only be "read" by a specially trained official known as a
quipucamayoc. The *quipu* comprises one main string, to which several
other strings are attached. Each string has a range of knots tied along
its length. With so many variations, these *quipu* could hold accurate
details about the whole Inca Empire. There were also *quipu* that
recorded the histories of the Inca leaders.

It is often true that great civilizations are held
together by a shared religion. The Inca, of
course, shared beliefs with their predecessors in
the Andes, and with the other peoples around
them, but they also had their own gods and religious
rituals. According to the first Spanish observers, the
Inca were deeply involved with ceremonies and
religious images and sacrifices. Their gods included the

Quipu

The Inca used a system of recording
information—such as details of
rulers, armies, or supplies of gold—
on a *quipu* (shown left). This was
made up of a length of string, or
cord, from which several other strings
were suspended. A range of knots
was then tied to each string, or sub-
string. Depending on the color and
position of both the strings and the
knots, a range of precise information
could be recorded. If a string was red,
for example, it referred to soldiers; if
it was yellow, it referred to gold.

POSITION OF KNOTS

*The number of knots closest to the
top denoted thousands (2,000)*

*The number of knots here denoted
how many hundreds (400)*

*This number denoted tens (60).
The total represented here is 2,460.
Individual digits would be last.*

TYPES OF KNOTS

Long knot
(four turns)

Single knot

Figure-
eight knot

creator god named Viracocha, but the true father of the Inca was the god of the sun, known as Inti. The Inca believed themselves to be the children of the sun. There was a great god of thunder. The moon was a woman, Mama Kilya. There was also a lord of lightning and a lord of earthquakes.

There were also innumerable local shrines where the gods of earth and water were venerated. There were hills and springs and rocks that were considered to be holy. The Inca loved to go on pilgrimages to these blessed places, where they made offerings of food or seashells. They knew they had to treat their gods with respect or they might be punished with an illness or a

SUN WORSHIPER
This stone at Machu Picchu was known as Intihuatana or the "hitching post of the sun." It worked as a solar clock on which the Inca could see the shadows of the sun and work out the day of the winter solstice (June 21) for their Festival of the Sun.

FESTIVAL OF THE SUN
The sun god Inti was the patron god of the Inca Empire, of the city of Cuzco, and of the line of Inca emperors who claimed descent from him. The most important ceremony, led by the Inca himself, was the Inti Raymi, the Festival of the Sun. The festival is still held each year on 24th June.

Mummies

The people of South America believed that after they died, they would go on living in another world. To this end, the bodies of their dead were often saved as mummies. As early as 3000 BCE, people preserved the bodies of their ancestors by drying them in the sun. The Inca believed their dead king was a god and that by worshiping his mummy, they would keep his soul alive. The Spanish burned all the mummies of the Inca rulers.

This Chavin culture mummy dates back to about 1000 BCE. The dead person was usually placed in a sitting position with their knees drawn up against their chest.

This is a Chimu mummy bundle from about 1000 CE. It contains a crouching body wrapped in layers of fine cotton and wool cloth. The head is false.

This Inca child was offered as a mountaintop sacrifice in about 1500 CE. The freezing air would have naturally mummified her.

poor harvest. The landscape was considered holy, and the soil beneath their feet was sacred. The sky above them was also sacred. Many animals were thought to be represented by the stars, similar to our own constellations. The Southern Cross, for example, represented a multicolored llama, the ancestor of all llamas. Stretching out from the capital city were shrines and stone pillars designed to chart the movement of the heavens.

Recent archaeological discoveries suggest that the Inca also practiced human sacrifice. It is not known exactly why these sacrifices were made—perhaps they marked an important event or were intended to ensure good rainfall. Archaeologists are continually discovering more about Inca sacrificial practices. Some think that the Inca, unlike the Aztecs, did not sacrifice many victims at a time. Instead, they believed that one perfect child was selected and then taken in procession to Cuzco where a great feast was held to honor the child and his or her family. Then the child was carried high up into the mountains to a specially built tomb. Here, with great ceremony, the victim was placed, wrapped in special clothes and surrounded by prized possessions from their life. It is not known if the child was killed before being walled into the tomb or left to die from the cold or starvation.

The Inca also held their long-dead ancestors in great respect. They worshiped them in their preserved state as mummies. To turn a dead body nto a mummy was a specialized task. First, the dead body was stripped of its internal organs and filled with a substance like tar. Next, the body was left outside to dry and harden in the natural forces of sun and frost. The mummy was then wrapped in sumptuous clothes and decorated with jewels and other precious objects. Sometimes a false head, with shells for eyes and a piece of wood for a nose, was placed on top of this rich bundle; a wig and a hat were occasionally added.

The mummies were not buried in tombs, like their Egyptian counterparts, but were placed in caves or the natural recesses of rocks. Some were even kept within the homes of their families to serve as a perpetual reminder of the people who had gone before. The mummies of the Inca leaders were seated on thrones of gold, in all the regalia of state, and the priests danced before them. In November, the month of the dead, the dead emperors were carried through the city in a religious procession.

The mummified lords and ladies, who were the ancestors of the various kinship groups, were honored in a similar fashion. A group of guardians, known as

BODIES FROM PERU
These two mummified figures are 500 years old. They were found in a desert cemetery in Peru, where the dry climate was ideal for drying out the bodies of the dead. High levels of natural salt in the soil have helped to preserve them.

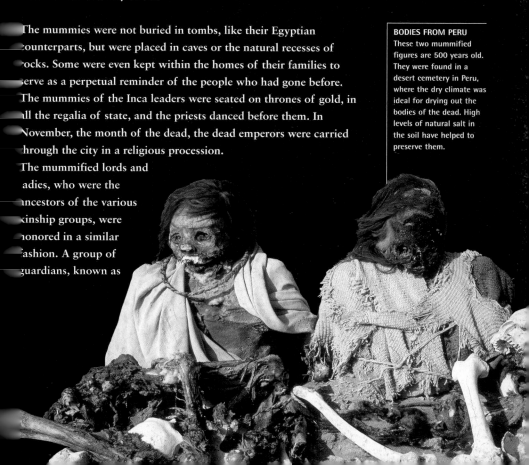

the *panaca*, preserved the estates and goods of the dead rulers. They maintained a staff of servants to care for their belongings.

FRANCISCO PIZARRO
The Spanish conquistador Francisco Pizarro (1475–1541) seized the Inca empire and claimed most of South America for Spain. He died in Peru, assassinated by a disgruntled faction of his men. This bronze statue of Pizarro was erected in his birthplace, Trujillo, Spain. An exact replica stands in the Peruvian capital, Lima.

But if these mummies were the preservers of the sacred soil, they were not powerful enough to withstand the force of the Spanish invasion. By the use of arms, and of treachery, the Spanish forces gradually took control of the kingdom. The Spanish conquistador Francisco Pizarro undertook three expeditions to Peru, lured by reports of fabulous riches to be found in some mysterious southern civilization. The arrival of the Europeans coincided with a smallpox epidemic in the region. The native people had no natural resistance to this foreign disease, and they died by the millions. The epidemic also carried off the Inca emperor, Huayna Capac, in 1525. After his death, two of his sons, Huáscar and Atahualpa, both laid claim to the throne.

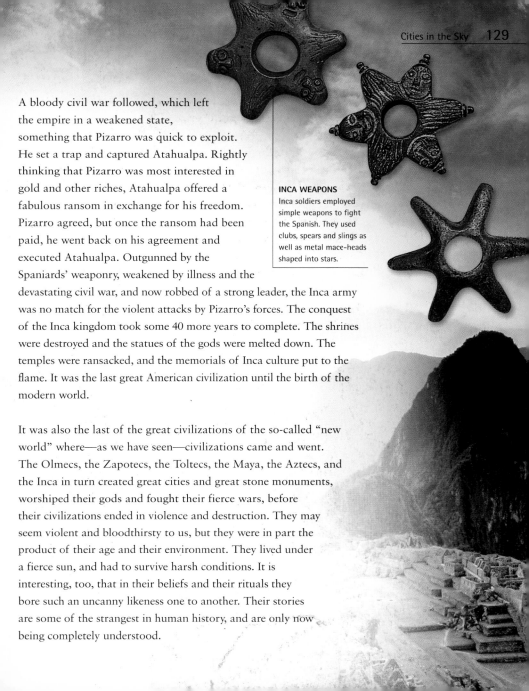

A bloody civil war followed, which left
the empire in a weakened state,
something that Pizarro was quick to exploit.
He set a trap and captured Atahualpa. Rightly
thinking that Pizarro was most interested in
gold and other riches, Atahualpa offered a
fabulous ransom in exchange for his freedom.
Pizarro agreed, but once the ransom had been
paid, he went back on his agreement and
executed Atahualpa. Outgunned by the
Spaniards' weaponry, weakened by illness and the
devastating civil war, and now robbed of a strong leader, the Inca army
was no match for the violent attacks by Pizarro's forces. The conquest
of the Inca kingdom took some 40 more years to complete. The shrines
were destroyed and the statues of the gods were melted down. The
temples were ransacked, and the memorials of Inca culture put to the
flame. It was the last great American civilization until the birth of the
modern world.

INCA WEAPONS
Inca soldiers employed
simple weapons to fight
the Spanish. They used
clubs, spears and slings as
well as metal mace-heads
shaped into stars.

It was also the last of the great civilizations of the so-called "new
world" where—as we have seen—civilizations came and went.
The Olmecs, the Zapotecs, the Toltecs, the Maya, the Aztecs, and
the Inca in turn created great cities and great stone monuments,
worshiped their gods and fought their fierce wars, before
their civilizations ended in violence and destruction. They may
seem violent and bloodthirsty to us, but they were in part the
product of their age and their environment. They lived under
a fierce sun, and had to survive harsh conditions. It is
interesting, too, that in their beliefs and their rituals they
bore such an uncanny likeness one to another. Their stories
are some of the strangest in human history, and are only now
being completely understood.

Reference
section

Timeline

THE GREAT CIVILIZATIONS of the early Americas existed for some 3,000 years. They centered around stone cities and grew large by conquering surrounding peoples. However, many of these empires existed side by side, trading with each other and absorbing styles of art and architecture. Many even shared similar gods and the same religious rituals.

Teotihuacan

Located in the central highlands of Mexico, Teotihuacan existed from 150–750 CE, and was the greatest of all Mesoamerican cities. The streets were laid out on a grid system with temples and palaces lining the main routes. Teotihuacan was deliberately destroyed in the 8th century CE, its temples burned and its palaces destroyed. The origins of its people are not known.

Terracotta bird ornament found in Teotihuacan

Olmecs

The Olmecs, who came from around the Gulf of Mexico, created the area's first great civilization. They flourished from 1200 to 300 BCE, and are known for their early form of writing and colossal head sculptures. They also controlled a rich trade in precious materials, such as jade. The civilization came to a violent end, the details of which remain unclear.

Olmec figure of a baby

Toltecs

From about 850 to 1200 CE, after the decline of Teotihuacan, the Toltecs controlled central Mexico. They built their capital city, Tula, and expanded their empire by going to war with their neighbors. It is thought that their power ended at the hands of the Aztecs.

A Toltec warrior looks out from a mask decorated with shells.

Toltec coyote mask

Zapotecs

The Zapotecs, from Mexico's southern highlands, flourished from 600 BCE to 800 CE, but were at their most powerful in about 200 BCE. This is when a massive workforce was organized to build the great city of Monte Alban with its pyramids and plazas, palaces and ball courts. Although never completely abandoned, the city declined after 800 CE. It was later absorbed by the Aztec Empire.

Stone temples at Monte Alban were once brightly painted.

1200 BCE	1100 BCE	1000 BCE	900 BCE	800 BCE	700 BCE	600 BCE	500 BCE	400 BCE	300 BCE	200 BCE	100 BCE	0	100 CE	200 CE
Olmecs														

This timeline shows how many early American civilizations lasted for centuries, and how some of them also existed alongside each other. The Aztec, Mixtec, and Inca civilizations ended abruptly when they were conquered by the Spanish.

Mixtecs

The Mixtecs succeeded the Zapotecs in the southern highlands of Mexico and were at their peak from about 800 CE until the Spanish conquest in 1521 CE. The Mixtecs founded new centers and also rebuilt some Zapotec cities. They were skilled in the use of metals, especially gold and silver. They also left historical records.

Pendant showing a Mesoamerican god

Maya

Two million Maya people once lived in 40 city-states around the Yucatán area of Mexico. These cities had ceremonial centers with spectacular pyramids, temples, and palaces. Some cities survived for centuries, from 250 BCE until the 1600s. The Maya invented their own system of writing to record their history and were also clever mathematicians. Their cities fell into a slow decline or were abandoned.

Maya children were often buried in pottery urns.

Aztecs

The Aztecs were a fierce tribe of warriors who settled on Lake Texcoco in the Valley of Mexico. Their capital at Tenochtitlán was an island city crisscrossed by canals. They built a great pyramid temple in the city center that became the site of many ritual human sacrifices to the sun god. The Aztec empire was based on military power and long-distance trade and flourished from 1250 CE until the Spanish conquest in 1521 CE.

Terra-cotta sculpture of an Aztec priest

The beads of this necklace are hollow gold.

Gold necklace found at Tenochtitlán

Inca

Many South American cultures thrived in the Andes before the Inca fought their way into the area around Cuzco in about 1100 CE. Over the next 400 years, the Inca expanded their territory. They built an intricate network of roads to link the distant parts of their empire. They were conquered by the Spanish in 1532.

Feather headdresses were worn by Inca nobles.

300 CE	400 CE	500 CE	600 CE	700 CE	800 CE	900 CE	1000 CE	1100 CE	1200 CE	1300 CE	1400 CE	1500 CE	1600 CE	1700 CE
				Zapotecs										
	Teotihuacan						Toltecs				Aztecs			
											Mixtecs			
						Maya								
									Inca					

Clues to the past

RCHAEOLOGISTS WORK LIKE DETECTIVES, finding and analyzing as many clues about their chosen people or site as they can. These clues can be the artifacts that they discover during a dig, the documents written by ancient people, or even human remains. All of these sources ovide fascinating information, which archaeologists piece together like a huge, but often incomplete, jigsaw puzzle.

Finding the evidence

During a dig, archaeologists need to record the precise location of every find. One way to do this is to make a grid, label each find, and then mark them clearly on a drawing of the grid for future reference. The position in which an artifact is found can tell experts a lot about the age and purpose of both the object and the surrounding area.

An archaeologist labels areas on a grid at Teotihuacan

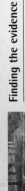

Skeletons and teeth

Archaeologists have excavated many graves to learn about people from their skeletons. The condition of bones and teeth can often provide details about what people ate and how they died. The size of the bones also helps experts to assess a person's age at death. Some skulls are clearly Maya because the shape shows evidence of cranial reshaping, or head-binding.

Maya female skull from the city of Copán

Map key

Olmecs The extent of the Olmec area of influence in about 1000 BCE.

Maya The area covered by the main Maya city-states in about 900 CE.

Aztecs The extent of the Aztec Empire at its height in about 1520 CE.

Incas By 1500 CE the Inca Empire stretched almost the entire length of South America.

Gulf of Mexico

Yucatán Peninsula

La Venta

Copán

Teotihuacan
Tenochtitlán

Pottery

A technique called thermoluminescence (TL) can show whether a pottery find is an ancient original or a modern fake. Archaeologists gently heat pieces of pottery. If certain minerals are present, they will release absorbed radiation in the form of light. This reveals the true date of the piece.

Zapotec-style pottery figure, revealed to be a fake

An artist draws a fragment of pottery

Finds from Copán in a special storage center

Storing and recording

Documentation is crucial when artifacts are discovered. Archaeologists make a record of the items, carefully noting where they were found. Artists may also illustrate the items. This information may be published for others to view, either in print or on the Internet. Similarly, artifacts must be stored. Some go on display in museums, but usually there are too many to exhibit. The rest are archived so they are not damaged any further.

Carbon dating

Material from the bodies of the dead, including bone, contains radioactive carbon that decays at a known rate. Scientists can measure how much of this carbon a bone sample contains, and then estimate the age of the remains.

ANDES   MOUNTAINS

South America

ANDES   MOUNTAINS

Machu
Picchu ■ ■ Cuzco

PACIFIC OCEAN

0   250   500   750   1,000 km

0   250   500   750   1,000 miles

Written records

Several Mesoamerican cultures, including the Maya, Mixtecs, and Aztecs, created written scripts made up of picturelike symbols called glyphs. It took scholars years to decode the glyphs, but now that most have been deciphered, they provide an insight into the lives of these people, including birth and death dates of rulers, as well as battles and major events.

A 6th-century stone with Maya glyphs

Aztec folding book written on bark paper

Modern techniques

High-tech techniques normally used by doctors on hospital patients can also be useful to learn about the past. For example, three-dimensional X-ray pictures produced by a computer topography (CT) scanner can reveal hidden details about mummies. This method offers an internal view, while the mummy remains intact. A scan of this mummified Inca girl found a fatal fracture to the skull. She may have been killed during a ritual sacrifice.

Fracture caused by a blow to the head

CT scan of Inca girl found in the Andes

Experts prepare to scan the mummified body.

Ancient rulers

THE KINGS OF THE Maya, Aztecs, and Inca ruled over great cities, where they built temples and palaces to demonstrate their power and wealth. Many rulers believed they were direct descendants of the gods. To expand their empires, the rulers went to war, seizing land and a captive workforce.

PAKAL THE GREAT
This is the death mask of Hanab Pakal, who ruled the city-state of Palenque. At the start of his reign, enemies attacked the city and killed many people. Pakal fought off his foes and went on to create a beautiful city.

Maya rulers

By around 250 CE, the land of the Maya was divided into many separate city-states. Each state governed itself and had its own ruling family. Although we know the names of many of these kings, the records are incomplete. The rulers tried to expand their power through warfare, as well as controlling the trade in precious stones and ordering carved inscriptions as a permanent record their victories.

(Numbers in parentheses show where scholars are uncertain about details)

Tikal

ORDER	NAME OF RULER	KNOWN DATES
1	Yax Moch Xok	c. 1st century CE
(2-13)	Rulers Unknown	
14	Great Jaguar Paw (Chak Tok Ich'ak)	317–378
(15)	Curl Nose (Nun Yax Ayin I)	379–?
16	Stormy Sky (Siyah Chan K'awil)	411–456
(17)	Kan Boar (K'an Chitam)	c. 475
(18)	Jaguar Paw Skull (Chak Tok Ich'ak II)	c. 488
19	Curl Head (Kalomte Balam)	c. 527
20	Unknown	
21	Double Bird (Wak Chan K'awil)	537–?
22	Animal Skull	c. 590
23	Unknown	
24	Unknown	
(25)	Shield Skull (Nun Uhol Chak)	c. 657–679
(26)	Hasaw Chan K'awil I	682–734?
27	Yik'in Chan K'awil	734–?
28	Unknown	
29	Chitam (Nun Yax Ayin II)	768–?
(30)	Dark Sun	810?
(31)	Hasaw Chan K'awil II	869?
	Last known ruler of Tikal	

Copán

ORDER	NAME OF RULER	KNOWN DATES
1	Yax K'uk Mo	426–c. 436
2	Popol K'inich	c. 436–?
3	Unknown	?–485
4	Cu Ix	485–c. 495
5	Unknown	
6	Unknown	
7	Waterlily Jaguar	c. early 6th century
8	Unknown	
9	Unknown	
10	Moon Jaguar	553–578
11	Butz' Chan (Smoke Serpent, Smoke Sky)	578–628
12	Smoke Jaguar (Smoke-Imix-God K)	628–695
13	18 Rabbit (Waxaklahun Ubah)	695–738
14	Smoke Monkey (738-749)	
15	Smoke Shell (Smoke Squirrel)	749–763
16	Yax Pac (Sun-at-Horizon)	763–820
–	U Cit Tok—Pretender to the throne, attempted to found a new dynasty in 822 but failed.	

Palenque

ORDER	NAME OF RULER	KNOWN DATES
1	K'uk' Balam *(Jaguar Quetzal)*	431–?
2	Casper	435–?
3	Butz'ah Sak Chik	487–?
4	Akal Mo'Nab I	501–524
5	K'an Hoy Chitam I	529–565
6	Akal Mo'Nab II	565–570
7	Kan Balam I	572–58
8	Lady Ol Ik'nal	583–604
9	Ah Neh Ol Mat	605–612
10	Lady Sak K'uk (Resplendent Quetzal)	612–615
11	Hanab Pakal (Pakal the Great)	615–683
12	Kan Balam II	684–702
13	K'an Hoy Chitam II	702–711

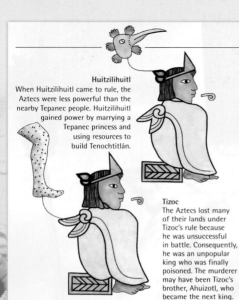

Huitzilihuitl
When Huitzilihuitl came to rule, the Aztecs were less powerful than the nearby Tepanec people. Huitzilihuitl gained power by marrying a Tepanec princess and using resources to build Tenochtitlán.

Tizoc
The Aztecs lost many of their lands under Tizoc's rule because he was unsuccessful in battle. Consequently, he was an unpopular king who was finally poisoned. The murderer may have been Tizoc's brother, Ahuitzotl, who became the next king.

Aztec rulers

Warriors were so important in Aztec society that each king had to begin his rule on the battlefield, adding cities and provinces to the empire, and capturing prisoners for ritual sacrifice. Rulers built newer and bigger temples to show their success.

ORDER	NAME OF RULER	KNOWN DATES
1	Acamapichtli (Handful of Reeds)	1372–1391
2	Huitzilihuitl (Hummingbird Feather)	1391–1415
3	Chimalpopoca (Smoking Shield)	1415–1426
4	Itzcoatl (Obsidian Serpent)	1426–1440
5	Moctezuma I (Angry Lord, Archer in the Sky)	1440–1468
6	Axayacatl (Water Face)	1468–1481
7	Tizoc (Chalk Leg)	1481–1486
8	Ahuitzotl (Water beast)	1486–1502
9	Moctezuma II (Angry Lord, the Younger)	1502–1520
10	Cuitlahuac	1520
11	Cuauhtemoc (Descending Eagle)	1520–1525

Inca rulers

Little is known about the first rulers of Cuzco. Some were mythical figures, and early writers disagree about the details of their reigns. More information exists on the later kings, who expanded the Inca territory along the coast of Peru.

The Kingdom of Cuzco

ORDER	NAME OF RULER	KNOWN DATES
1	Manco Capac	
2	Sinchi Roca	
3	Lloque Yupanqui	
4	Maita Capac	
5	Capac Yupanqui	
6	Inca Roca	
7	Yahuar Huacac	
8	Inca Viracocha	died 1438

The Inca Empire

ORDER	NAME OF RULER	KNOWN DATES
9	Pachacuti-Inca	1438–1471
10	Topa Inca Yupanqui	1471–1493
11	Huayna Capac	1493–1527
12	Huascar (ruled the south)	1527–1532
13	Atahualpa (ruled the north)	1527–1533

Inca Viracocha
Named after the main creator-god, Inca Viracocha ruled before the empire was established. He was determined to create an empire that stretched beyond Cuzco, so he began to conquer the area outside the city, and left officials to rule these new lands. His work was carried on at a much faster rate by Pachacuti.

Pyramids

THE CIVILIZATIONS OF Mesoamerica left a legacy of spectacular pyramids. These varied in size and design but were usually the most important buildings in a city, rising high above the surrounding palaces, houses, and plazas. Pyramids were sometimes built over the tombs of rulers and often had temple buildings at the top, reached by means of an outer stairway.

Teotihuacan pyramids

The first great city in Mesoamerica was Teotihuacan. Its main avenue was lined with pyramids, including the Pyramid of the Sun and the Pyramid of the Moon.

Pyramid of the Sun
TEOTIHUACAN (1–150 CE)
Built over the site of a sacred cave, this pyramid was the third-largest ever built.
Height: 207 ft (63 m)

Five stepped platforms

East facade faces the rising sun.

West facade faces the setting sun.

Aztec pyramids

The ceremonial center of Tenochtitlán was enclosed by a masonry wall decorated with serpent heads. The center was dominated by the Great Temple, site of ritual sacrifices.

Great Temple
TENOCHTITLÁN (c. 1390 CE)
The pyramid that supported the twin temples was rebuilt seven times. As with other Aztec pyramids, it featured two staircases up one side.
Height: 197 ft (60 m)

Twin temples

Victims for sacrifice were led up 114 steps.

Curved design

Temple of Quetzalcoatl
TENOCHTITLÁN (c. 1390 CE)
This stone temple was dedicated to the feathered serpent god. Its circular side is an unusual feature
Height: not known

Maya pyramids

The Maya created highly decorated pyramids and temples. The height of the pyramids emphasized the importance of priests performing sacred rituals in the temple at the top.

Pyramid of the Giant Jaguar
TIKAL (c. 700 CE)
The grandeur of this pyramid represented the wealth and success of Tikal at the time. The chamber at the top served to amplify the voices of priests.
Height: 145 ft (44 m)

Entrance to temple chamber

Temple of the Inscriptions
PALENQUE (c. 650 CE)
This temple was built by Pakal the Great, and his tomb was hidden at the base of the pyramid. The carved inscriptions in the temple tell of his achievements.
Height: 75 ft (23 m)

A trap door in the temple floor led down to Pakal's tomb.

Main Temple
XPUHIL (c. 700 CE)
This Maya temple has solid stone towers with external stairways. These are so steep that they were probably just built for decorative purposes.
Height: not known

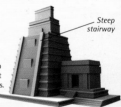

Steep stairway

Pyramid of the Magician
UXMAL (c. 900 CE)
The sides of this unusual oval temple are covered with smooth slabs of limestone. Legend has it that it was built by the Maya god Itzamna.
Height: 100 ft (30 m)

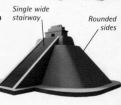

Single wide stairway

Rounded sides

El Castillo
CHICHÉN ITZÁ (c. 1100 CE)
This nine-level pyramid is decorated with feathered snakes and dedicated to Kukulkan, who was the Maya equivalent of the feathered serpent Quetzalcoatl.
Height: 79 ft (24 m)

There was a stairway on each of the four sides.

Ancient gods

THE MAYA, AZTECS, AND INCA all worshiped a range of gods. While some of these were powerful figures thought to have created the entire universe, others had control over specific aspects of life, including war and learning. Gods and goddesses of nature, in particular of the rain and sun, were popular because they helped crops to grow.

Aztec gods

Chicometcoatl

Ometeotl
The supreme Aztec god Ometeotl could take both male and female forms. In female form, Ometeotl gave birth to many other gods.

Huitzilopochtli
As sun god, Huitzilopochtli was reborn at sunrise every day. He was also the god of war and was often portrayed as a fearless warrior.

Quetzalcoatl
The feathered serpent Quetzalcoatl was god of three things—wind, priesthood, and learning. The Aztecs believed he invented the calendar.

Tezcatlipoca
The name of this god means "smoking mirror." Tezcatlipoca had a mirror in which he could see the future.

Quetzalcoatl

Tlaloc
As god of rain and fertility, Tlaloc made the crops grow. However, he was dangerous because he also caused storms.

Xipe Totec
Priests of the springtime god Xipe Totec wore the flayed skins taken from sacrificial victims. Removing the old skin was a sign that spring had arrived.

Xochiquetzal
Worshipers of Xochiquetzal brought flowers to this flower, fruit, and music goddess.

Chicometcoatl
The corn god was Chicometcoatl, and she guarded the seeds that were kept for sowing each year.

Maya gods

Chac

Itzamna
This god resembled an old man with a hooked nose. He was very powerful because he was lord of day and night. The Maya believed he invented writing.

Ix Chel
The wife of Itzamna, Ix Chel controlled pregnancy, childbirth, and fertility. She gave life and kept the bones and souls of the deceased. In addition, she had the power to tell the future.

Ah Puch
Widely feared, Ah Puch was the god of death. He was said to take away the souls of the dying.

Chac
A steady stream of tears flowed from Chac's eyes. These fell to earth and helped the plants to grow—he was the rain god.

Ixtab
There was a goddess of suicide. Ixtab dangled from the sky with

a rope around her neck, ready to grab the souls of anyone who had killed themselves.

Kukulcan
The Maya god of the winds was a feathered serpent called Kukulcan. He was similar to the Aztec god Quetzalcoatl.

Nacon
Maya warriors respected Nacon, the god of war. His festival was celebrated every year in May.

Inca gods

Inti
The sun god Inti was the most powerful of all the Inca gods. He was portrayed with a human face and had rays of bright sunlight streaming from his head. The temple of the sun in Cuzco was dedicated to him. Inti was also known as Puncha, but when he took on this form, he was shown as a warrior armed with darts.

Copacati
As goddess of lakes, Copacati was said to have submerged the temples of the other gods beneath the water. She was worshiped at Lake Titicaca.

Ilyap'a
The thunder god Ilyap'a fired stones at a pot of water. The sound of the stones made the noise of thunder and the water splashes were the raindrops.

Kon
A son of Inti, Kon was the Inca god of rain and the south wind.

Mama Cocha
The water goddess Mama Cocha controlled the oceans and rivers. Inca along the Pacific coastline prayed to her for calm seas.

Vichama
God of death and another son of Inti, Vichama brought destruction

to people. He also produced a clutch of eggs from which a new group of people hatched.

Sun god, Inti

Glossary

Words in *italics* have their own entry in the glossary.

A

Alliance An association or bond between two groups based on shared interests and aims.

Allyu The name for an *Inca* family group.

Ancestor A family relative from the distant past.

Appease To keep someone happy or satisfied; for example, offering *sacrifices* appeased the gods.

Aqueduct A structure, usually raised, with a pipe or channel for transporting water from one place to another.

Archaeology The study of past human life and *culture* by recovering and examining material evidence, such as buildings and pottery. Practiced by archaeologists.

Aztec A *Mesoamerican civilization* that established the city of Tenochtitlán, and existed from approximately 1200 CE until the Spanish *conquest* in 1521 CE. Also the name of the people who lived there.

B

Ball game A *ritual* game, played by various Mesoamerican peoples, on special ball courts. Losers were sometimes *sacrificed* to the gods.

Barter To trade or exchange items without using money.

Bloodletting *Ritual* cutting or piercing of the human body to produce blood as an offering to the gods.

C

Calmecac An *Aztec* school for children from noble families. Ordinary children went to the *telpochcalli*.

Calpullec The leader of the *calpulli*.

Calpulli An *Aztec* group of people or a clan, linked by family or trade. The word means "group of houses."

Cannibalism The practice by humans of eating human flesh.

Caste A social class separated from the rest of a society, such as a priestly caste.

Cataclysm A momentous event marked by upheaval and destruction—often a violent force of nature, such as a flood or an earthquake.

Causeway A raised road, usually built over water. The *Aztec* city of Tenochtitlán was an island with causeways connecting it to the mainland.

Cenote A natural well used as a source of water and considered sacred by the *Maya*.

Chacmool Stone sculpture of a reclining human holding a basin, used during human *sacrifices*.

Chasquis *Inca* state messengers who carried goods and information across the empire.

Chicha *Inca* beer made from corn.

Chichimeca An invading northern tribe who may have destroyed the *Toltec Empire*.

City-state A state ruled by one city. The *Maya Empire* was divided into city-states, each with its own king and ruling family.

Civilization An organized and advanced society with its own systems of record-keeping and government.

Codex A long strip of paper folded in accordion-style pages to form a book (plural: codices).

Colla Stone storehouses along the *Inca* road networks that contained food for travelers.

Colony A group of people who live some distance from the ruler but are still under his command.

Conquest Act of conquering; for example, taking charge of a city after winning a war.

Cult A religious group or community with its own set of *rituals* and beliefs.

Culture Patterns of behavior, beliefs, and ideals associated with a group of people.

D

Decipher To read and interpret a code or system of writing, such as *hieroglyphics*.

Deity A god with powers over the natural world.

Demise The gradual end of an existence or activity.

Desecrate To destroy something that is *sacred*.

Domesticate To tame a wild animal or plant so that humans can use or live with it.

E

Edifice An important building, such as a temple or a palace.

Effigy An image or statue that represents a particular person.

Elite A group or class of people who hold the highest status within a society.

Empire People and land that are governed solely by one ruler, including distant *colonies*.

Epidemic The outbreak of a disease that spreads rapidly through a population.

Ethics A set of guidelines on the right and wrong ways to behave in a society.

G H

Genealogy The study of a family history to trace *ancestors*.

Glyph A mark or symbol that represents ideas or images.

Hierarchy A system in which society is separated into different ranks depending on ability or status, ranging from the *elite* to the *serfs*.

Hieroglyph A picture of a person, animal, or object that is used as a form of writing to record information.

Hybrid A combination of different characteristics; for example, many *deities* were part-human, part-animal.

I J K

Inca An *empire* that covered modern-day Peru, Bolivia, Ecuador, Colombia, Chile, and parts of Argentina. Also the name of the people who lived there. The *Inca Empire* flourished from 1438 CE until Spanish conquest in 1532 CE.

Izapan People who occupied an area of land between the *Olmecs* and the *Maya*, who traded and spread ideas between the two groups.

Kinship A close *alliance* often involving a connection between groups through marriage.

K'ul ahaw The *Maya* word for a holy lord.

L

Laceration A flesh wound caused by piercing or cutting the skin. An *Aztec ritual* involved self-laceration to offer blood to the gods.

Legend A story handed down from one generation to the next that refers to a historical event, though the details may have been exaggerated.

Litter A comfortable chair or couch with handles, used to carry an important person.

Long Count A *Maya* counting system used to record dates.

M

Macabre Anything gruesome and associated with death.

Maguey A Mexican plant of the cactus family used to make coarse clothing.

Manioc A starchy root vegetable used to make a type of flour.

Maya A *Mesoamerican civilization* that flourished from approximately 1000 BCE and whose great cities went into decline in the 16th century. Some *Maya* customs and language have survived.

Mercenary A soldier who is hired to fight for his own or another group or country.

Meridian An imaginary circle that runs from north to south around Earth. When certain stars crossed the meridian, the *Aztecs* would perform ritual *sacrifices*.

Mesoamerica A region extending through central Mexico, and including parts of Guatemala, Belize, Honduras, and El Salvador.

Mexica An earlier name for the *Aztecs*.

Militaristic A society focussed on military activities, such as wars with rival groups.

Mit'a service A period of time when able men had to help on projects for the good of the *Inca Empire*, such as construction work or repairing roads and bridges.

Mitmacs Groups of people forced by the *Inca* emperor to move to newly conquered lands.

Mummy A dead body that is specially preserved and embalmed before burial.

Mural A picture painted directly onto a wall.

Myth A traditional story that may or may not be true but is believed by a group of people to be real. Myths usually involve gods and explain creation and the natural world.

N O

Nahuatl The language of the *Aztecs*, still spoken in parts of central America.

Nomadic People with no fixed home who travel from place to place in search of grazing land for their animals, and food and water for themselves.

Observatory A building from which the planets and stars are observed in the night sky.

Obsidian Black, volcanic glasslike rock often used to make sharp tools and weapons.

Olmec The first great *civilization* of *Mesoamerica*, which flourished from approximately 1200 to 300 BCE.

Omen A sign or *prophecy* of good or bad future events.

P

Panaca A group of *Inca* guardians who preserved the lands and goods of dead rulers.

Pilgrimage A journey to a holy place.

Placate To please and pacify. Human *sacrifice* was practiced to placate the gods.

Pok-a-Tok The *Maya* word for the *ritual ball game*.

Popol Vuh The name of a collection of *Maya myths* and *legends* that was written down in Spanish. The original book has disappeared.

Primitive Simple and unsophisticated, associated with early societies of people.

Processional An avenue wide enough for a procession of people to travel down.

Prophecy A future prediction made by consulting the gods.

Q R

Quadrant A section of land that has been divided into four equal sections.

Quechua The language of the *Inca*. Also their name until the Spanish renamed them *Inca*. The Quechua only named their king "Inca," which means supreme being.

Quetzal A central American bird whose brilliant red and bronze-green feathers were used by the *Aztecs* to make headdresses, shields, and other forms of decoration.

Quipu An *Inca* system of recording information using various colors of knotted strings.

Quipucamayoc An *Inca* official trained to "read" and understand the language of knots.

Reciprocity An agreement between people to exchange items and favors with one another.

Regalia Anything associated with royalty, including fine foods and clothing.

Retinue The people who attend to the needs of an emperor.

Ritual Special rules and methods of a religious procedure such as a *sacrifice*.

S

Sacred Anything that is associated with a religious *deity*, such as a temple, an object, or a way of behaving.

Sacrifice An offering to a *deity*, usually involving a *ritual* killing of a human or animal.

Sarcophagus A stone coffin, usually with pictures and *hieroglyphs* carved into the lid. The sarcophagus of an important ruler would usually be kept in a *sacred* building.

Scepter A ceremonial staff held by a ruler to symbolize his or her authority.

Scribe A person who is specially trained to write and record events.

Septum The thin wall that separates the two nostrils. The *Aztec* ruler, Moctezuma II, wore a huge emerald in his septum.

Serf A type of slave, given the lowest status in a society.

Shaman A spiritual leader, thought to have magical powers, who acts as a medium between the real and spirit worlds.

Shrine A holy place or a container for *sacred* relics.

Stela A large carved or inscribed stone slab, found in ruined *Maya* cities (plural: stelae).

Subjugate To forcefully defeat and conquer a rival ruler.

Syllable A unit of sound. The word *Aztec* has two syllables—"Az" and "tec."

T

Tahuantinsuyu The name given by the Inca to their *empire*. The word means "the Land of the Four Quarters" because the empire was divided into from quadrants.

Tambos Lodging houses and taverns along the *Inca* roads, where *chasquis* could rest.

Tapir A central American animal related to the horse and rhinoceros, with short legs and a fleshy snout.

Telpochcalli An *Aztec* school for training the sons of tradesmen and peasants. This type of school did not teach reading or writing.

Tepanec A tribe who were defeated by the *Aztecs* and who later formed an alliance with the Spanish.

Tlachtli The *Aztec* word for the *ritual ball game*.

Tlatoani A word used to describe an *Aztec* ruler, literally translated as "he who speaks."

Tlaxcalan An independent tribe who the Spanish defeated on their marched toward the *Aztecs*.

Toltec A *militaristic civilization* who lived in the city of Tula from 950 to 1150.

Tribute A gift or honor given to a ruler or *deity*.

Tzompantli The *Aztec* word for a skull-rack where decapitated heads of *sacrificed* victims were displayed.

V W Y Z

Vandalize To intentionally damage or destroy something that belongs to someone else.

Were-jaguar A famous *Olmec* image that is a *hybrid* creature, part-child and part-jaguar.

Yanas Servants of *Inca* nobles.

Zapotec A *Mesoamerican civilization* that thrived from approximately 600 BCE–800 CE.

Index

Credits

The publisher would like to thank the following for their kind permission to reproduce their photographs:

(Key: a=above; b=below; c=center; l=left; r=right; t=top)

1 Corbis: Macduff Everton. 2 Corbis: Macduff Everton tc; Robert Landau bc; Nik Wheeler bcr. Getty Images: Art Wolfe bcrr. 2-3 The Art Archive: Museo Regional de Oaxaca Mexico / Dagli Orti c. akg-images: François Guénet bcl. Corbis: br; Jim Erickson br; Brian A. Vikander bcrr. Werner Forman Archive: Museum fur Völkerkunde, Vienna bcll. Peter Newark's Military Pictures: bc. 4-5 Corbis: Archivo Iconografica, S.A. t; Michael & Patricia Fogden c. 5 Getty Images: Brent Stirton b. 6 N.H.P.A.: Andy Rouse crb. 6-7 Corbis: Robert Landau. 7 The Art Archive: National Anthropological Museum Mexico / Dagli Orti cb. Werner Forman Archive: Dallas Museum of Art, USA clb. 8 Corbis: Jonathan Blair bc. Getty Images: Rex Ziak tl. 8-9 Science Photo Library: Copyright 1995, Worldsat International and, J. Knighton (background). 9 DK Images: Alan Watson cra. N.H.P.A.: Andy Rouse br. 10 Corbis: Danny Lehman l. 10-11 Corbis: Danny Lehman. 11 Corbis: Staffan Widstrand br. DK Images: © CONACULTA-INAH-MEX. Authorized reproduction by the Instituto Nacional de Antropología e Historia t. Eye Ubiquitous: Elliot Walker br. 12 Corbis: Gianni Dagli Orti cla. 12-13 The Art Archive: National Anthropological Museum Mexico / Dagli Orti b. Getty Images: James Strachan t. 13 Werner Forman Archive: Dallas Museum of Art, USA br. 14 Corbis: Gianni Dagli Orti tl; DK Images: © CONACULTA-INAH-MEX. Authorized reproduction by the Instituto Nacional de Antropología e Historia bl, bl, bl. 14-15 Corbis: Craig Lovell t; Michele Westmorland b. 15 Corbis: Gianni Dagli Orti br. 16 Corbis: Danny Lehman crb; Nik Wheeler. 17 Corbis: Danny Lehman bc; Gianni Dagli Orti clb. 18 Dr. N.J.Saunders tl. Still Pictures: Keith Kent tc. 19 Corbis: Danny Lehman c; Charles & Josette Lenars br. 20-21 Corbis: Gianni Dagli Orti b. 21 Corbis: Gianni Dagli Orti tl. 22 DK Images: © CONACULTA-INAH-MEX. Authorized reproduction by the Instituto Nacional de Antropología e Historia tl. 22-23 Corbis: Randy Faris. 23 Werner Forman Archive: tr. 24 Corbis: Tom Brakefield cla. Getty Images: Tim Davis tr; Stuart Westmorland tl. 25 The Art Archive: Dagli Orti c. Werner Forman Archive: br. 26 Hutchison Library: Michael Macintyre tl. 26-27 Corbis: Danny Lehman. 28 Corbis: Gianni Dagli Orti crb. Getty Images: Art Wolfe. 29 The Art Archive: Museo Regional de Oaxaca Mexico / Dagli Orti clb. Peter Newark's Military Pictures: cb. 30 Corbis: David Muench l. DK Images: Natural History Museum tc, tc, tc. 31 Werner Forman Archive: Museum fur Völkerkunde, Basel br. 32 Corbis: Gianni Dagli Orti bl. 32-33 Corbis: David Muench b. 33 The Art Archive: tr. 34 Corbis: Bettmann cla, cl, clb. 34-35 Corbis: Hulton-Deutsch Collection t. 35 The Art Archive: Museo Regional de Oaxaca Mexico / Dagli Orti tr. 36 Corbis: Roger Ressmeyer tr. Werner Forman Archive: tl. National Geographic Image Collection: Filipe Davalos tl. 37 Corbis (background). Werner Forman Archive: br. Peter Newark's Military Pictures: tl. 38 The Art Archive: Museum für Völkerkunde Vienna / Dagli Orti bl. 39 Corbis: Archivo Iconografico, S.A. r. 40 Corbis: Jan Butchofsky-Houser l. 40-41 Corbis: Sergio Dorantes (background). Peter Newark's Military Pictures: b. 41 The Art Archive: Bodleian Library Oxford / The Bodleian Library tr. 43 Corbis: Amos Nachoum clb. Still Pictures: Martin Wendler cb. 44 Corbis: Gianni Dagli Orti tl. 46-47 Corbis: Amos Nachoum b. 47 Corbis: Sergio Pitamitz tr. 48 Corbis: Liba Taylor bl. Werner Forman Archive: National Museum of Anthropology, Mexico City. 49 Werner Forman Archive: National Museum of Anthropology, Mexico. Still Pictures: Martin Wendler b. 50 Corbis: Macduff Everton bl. 51 DK Images: © CONACULTA-INAH-MEX. Authorized reproduction by the Instituto Nacional de Antropología e Historia tr. 52 Corbis: Gianni Dagli Orti clb. 52-53 Corbis. 53 Corbis: Charles & Josette Lenars clb; Tim Pannell bc. 54 DK Images: © CONACULTA-INAH-MEX. Authorized reproduction by the Instituto Nacional de Antropología e Historia tl. 54-55 DK Images: Brian Cosgrove t. 55 DK Images: Michel Zabe b. 56 DK Images: © CONACULTA-INAH-MEX. Authorized reproduction by the Instituto Nacional de Antropología e Historia tl. The Art Archive: Biblioteca Nacional Madrid / Dagli Orti bl. 57 Corbis: Reuters bc. DK Images: © CONACULTA-INAH-MEX. Authorized reproduction by the Instituto Nacional de Antropología e Historia cl. 58 DK Images: © CONACULTA-INAH-MEX. Authorized reproduction by the Instituto Nacional de Antropología e Historia clb, cl, clb, bl; British Museum bl. 58-59 Corbis. 59 The Art Archive: tl. 60 The Art Archive: Museo del Templo Mayor Mexico / Dagli Orti tr. Werner Forman Archive: National Museum of Anthropology, Mexico City bl. 61 Corbis: Gianni Dagli Orti tr. 62 Corbis: Charles & Josette Lenars c. 63 Corbis: Tony Arruza br. 64 Werner Forman Archive: Smithsonian Institution, Washington ct. Science Photo Library: John Chumack tr. 64-65 Corbis: Tim Pannell. 66 DK Images: Michel Zabe clb. Werner Forman Archive: Museum fur Völkerkunde, Vienna. 67 Corbis: Kevin Fleming clb. 68-69 Corbis: Kevin Fleming. 69 DK Images: Michel Zabe cra. Werner Forman Archive: br. 70 Corbis: Gianni Dagli Orti cl. The Art Archive: Bodleian Library Oxford / The Bodleian Library tl, clb, crb, bl. 71 Corbis: Dave G. Houser b, r. Werner Forman Archive: tc; British Museum, London tl, tll. 72-73 Corbis: Galen Rowell. 73 Reuters: cr. 74 DK Images: Robin Wigington, Arbour Antiques tc. 75 Science Photo Library: Eye of Science tl. 76 akg-images: François Guénet. Corbis: Macduff Everton crb. 77 The Art Archive: Archaeological and Ethnological Museum Guatemala City / Dagli Orti cb. Robert Harding Picture Library: Robert Frerck/Odyssey br. 78 Corbis: Archivo Iconografico, S.A. tr; Charles & Josette Lenars b. 79 National Geographic Image Collection: Kenneth Garrett br. 80 The Art Archive: Archaeological Museum Copan Honduras / Dagli Orti b. DK Images: © CONACULTA-INAH-MEX. Authorized reproduction by the Instituto Nacional de Antropología e Historia bl. 81 Corbis: Macduff Everton t. 82 Werner Forman Archive: British Museum cl. 82-83 Robert Harding Picture Library: Robert Frerck/Odyssey. 83 Corbis: Gianni Dagli Orti br. 84 Corbis: Charles & Josette Lenars l. 85 The Art Archive: Archaeological and Ethnological Museum Guatemala City / Dagli Orti c. Corbis: Charles & Josette Lenars clb. 86 The Art Archive: Archaeological Museum Tikal Guatemala / Dagli Orti crb. Peter Newark's Military Pictures. 87 The Art Archive: Dagli Orti cb; Archaeological and Ethnological Museum Guatemala City / Dagli Orti clb. 88 DK Images: © CONACULTA-INAH-MEX. Authorized reproduction by the Instituto Nacional de Antropología e Historia tr. The Art Archive: Archaeological Museum Tikal Guatemala / Dagli Orti tl, bl, (background). 89 The Art Archive: Archaeological Museum Tikal Guatemala / Dagli Orti br. DK Images: © CONACULTA-INAH-MEX. Authorized reproduction by the Instituto Nacional de Antropología e Historia cl. Science Photo Library: Geoff Tompkinson b. 90 Photograph K4822G © Justin Kerr tl. Science Photo Library: Roger Harris bl; John Sanford (background). 90-91 Robert Harding Picture Library: Dale Sloat/Phototake NYC. 91 Werner Forman Archive: National Museum of Anthropology, Mexico bc. 92 The Art Archive: Archaeological and Ethnological Museum Guatemala City / Dagli Orti l. Corbis: Tom Ives (background). 93 Corbis: Jim Craigmyle r. 94 The Art Archive: Archaeological and Ethnological Museum Guatemala City / Dagli Orti cb. 95 The Art Archive: Dagli Orti. 97 Corbis: Archivo Iconografica, S.A. clb; Vanni Archive cb. DK Images: Brian Cosgrove clb (background). 99 DK Images: © CONACULTA-INAH-MEX. Authorized reproduction by the Instituto Nacional de Antropología e Historia tr. 100 Corbis: l (background); Gianni Dagli Orti tr. Werner Forman Archive: cl. Heather Magrill: bc. 101 Corbis: r. 102 Ancient Art & Architecture Collection: cla. The Art Archive: Xalapa Museum Veracruz Mexico / Dagli Orti bc. Corbis: Macduff Everton tl. 102-103 Corbis: Archivo Iconografico, S.A. b. DK Images: Brian Cosgrove (background). 103 Corbis: Charles & Josette Lenars br. World Pictures: tr. 104 Corbis: Danny Lehman c. 105 Corbis: Vanni Archive tc. Werner Forman Archive: National Museum of Anthropology, Mexico City cr. 106-107 Corbis: Dallas and John Heaton b. Science Photo Library: Keith Kent t. 107 Corbis: Lynsey Addario tr. DK Images: Brian Cosgrve b. 108 South American Pictures: Tony Morrison crb. 108-109 Corbis: Brian A. Vikander. 109 Corbis: Jeremy Horner cb; Galen Rowell clb. 110 DK Images: Royal Museum of Scotland bl. 110-111 Robert Harding Picture Library: R Frerck tr (background). 111 Corbis: Kevin Schafer bl. 112 South American Pictures: Tony Morrison tl. 112-113 South American Pictures: Tony Morrison (background). 113 DK Images: Cambridge Museum of Archaeology and Anthropology r. 114 Corbis: Charles & Josette Lenars cl. 114-115 Corbis: Chris Lisle. 115 Corbis: Galen Rowell tr. 116 Corbis: Chase Jarvis tc; Francesco Venturi cl. 116-117 Galen Rowell t. 117 Corbis: Wolfgang Kaehler cr. 118 Corbis: cl; Mark A. Johnson bl. DK Images: Royal Museum of Scotland tl. 119 Corbis: Jeremy Horner br. DK Images: Royal Museum of Scotland crb, br. 120 Corbis: Jim Erickson; J. C. Kanny / Lorpresse / Sygma crb. 121 Corbis: Bertrand Rieger / Museart / Sygma cb; Charles & Josette Lenars clb. 122 akg-images: Veintimilla l. Corbis: J. C. Kanny / Lorpresse / Sygma tl; Charles & Josette Lenars bl. 123 akg-images: Veintimilla r. National Geographic Image Collection: Maria Stenzel br. 124 Corbis: Pablo Corral Vega tl. DK Images: bl. 124-125 Corbis: Nevada Wier. 125 Corbis: Francesco Venturi tr. 126 Corbis: Galen Rowell cl. DK Images: Bolton Museum clb; Museum of Mankind c. National Geographic Image Collection: Johan Reinhard tc. 127 Robert Harding Picture Library: Chris Rennie b. Science Photo Library: John Sanford t. 128 Corbis: Bertrand Rieger / Museart / Sygma b. 129 Alamy Images: Galen Rowell/Mountain Light br. Copyright 2004 Smithsonian Institution: Mark Gulezian tr. 130-131 www.bridgeman.co.uk: Museum of Mankind, London, UK. 132 Corbis: Macduff Everton bl; Gianni Dagli Orti tr, cl. DK Images: © CONACULTA-INAH-MEX. Authorized reproduction by the Instituto Nacional de Antropología e Historia br. 132-133 Corbis: Dallas and John Heaton (background); Jim Zuckerman (background). 133 Corbis: Macduff Everton bc. DK Images: © CONACULTA-INAH-MEX. Authorized reproduction by the Instituto Nacional de Antropología e Historia tr. Werner Forman Archive: br; National Museum of Anthropology, Mexico City tr. 134 DK Images: British Museum br. National Geographic Image Collection: Kenneth Garrett c, cr. 135 DK Images: © CONACULTA-INAH-MEX. Authorized reproduction by the Instituto Nacional de Antropología e Historia. bl. Werner Forman Archive: c. National Geographic Image Collection: Kenneth Garrett tr, cla; Maria Stenzel cr, br. Science Photo Library: James King-Holmes r. 136 Alamy Images: Jamie Marshall c. Corbis: Sergio Dorantes tr. 136-137 Corbis: Kevin Schafer (background). 137 Alamy Images: Jamie Marshall b. Ancient Art & Architecture Collection: M. Jelliffe crb. Archivo Iconografico, S.A. r (background). 139 www.bridgeman.co.uk: Museum of Mankind, London, UK ca. DK Images: © CONACULTA-INAH-MEX. Authorized reproduction by the Instituto Nacional de Antropología e Historia clb, tr. South American Pictures: Tony Morrison br. 140-141 Corbis: Dallas and John Heaton. 142-143 Corbis: Dallas and John Heaton.

All other images © Dorling Kindersley.
For further information, see www.dkimages.com.

Dorling Kindersley would also like to thank:
Lee Gibbons for digital artworks on pages 42, 44-45, 74-75, 96-97, 98-99, 138; Kath Northam for illustration on page 79; Chris Bernstein for the index; Lee Simmons for proofreading; Sue Murdoch for additional research; Kate Bradshaw, Andrea Mills and Rosie O'Neill for editorial assistance.